FAITH PROMISE AND BEYOND

Unlocking the resources of the Church to help fulfill the Great Commission

D0170488

Keith Brown
with
John W. Hoover

First Edition
First Printing September 1995
Ninth Printing January 2003

Library of Congress Catalog Card Number: 95-83429
ISBN: 1-57502-101-3

Additional copies may be obtained by writing to:
Keith Brown
1630 Bluewater Ct.
Cumming, GA 30041

Printed in the USA by

MORRIS PUBLISHING
3212 East Highway 30 • Kearney, NE 68847 • 1-800-650-7888

Table of Contents

People often say, "I really would like to give to missions. But you know how it is. We have house payments, car payments, plastic card payments, children's education. We just never have enough money left over to give." Is it really a question of "just not having any money to give?" Or could it be something else? It helps to be reminded what we do spend on things such as wrinkle cream, peanut butter, sunglasses, sneakers, Christmas trees, etc. Suppose everyone gave to missions an amount equal to what they spend a year on these items. How much would that generate for missions? It helps to put things in perspective and get a sharper view of our financial priorities.

Tom Telford, ACMC regional director, was asked to list the churches in America that gave the largest amounts of money each year for missions. Twenty-three churches were listed. Twenty of the twenty-three use the Faith Promise plan. Most of these churches give in excess of $1 million a year to missions, using the Faith Promise plan. If my church is only giving a few thousand dollars (or less) a year for missions, and there are many other churches of similar size and financial means giving tens and even hundreds of thousands of dollars, there must be a reason. More times than not, that reason is Faith Promise.

An unexpected bonus for the exact amount of a Faith Promise, a rock thrown through a window years before, an unexpected check from a businessman, a nursery that buys a Japanese maple tree out of the yard of a woman who had made a faith commitment —these and many other examples show the varied ways God uses to enable His people to meet their Faith Promise commitments. Miraculous, out of the blue, unexpected.

When the Faith Promise plan is presented, the most misunderstood area is often in response to the question, "How will God supply my Faith Promise?" Many are confused when it is explained. Some are misinformed. Many times a particular experience is held up as the norm for all. How does God supply a Faith Promise? Another method God uses is the miracle of assisting us to gain control of our lifestyles and spending habits, even to the point of sacrifice.

5. Creative Giving

One couple raises berries, another lady uses her "gift" of making ceramics, a pastor's daughter delivers newspapers, an overweight salesman cuts out lunches and in the process loses weight and gains money for his Faith Promise, a teenager crochets bells to hang on Christmas trees. These and many others are examples of the third way God enables His people to meet their Faith Promise commitments — by using the creative skills God has given them.

6. History of the Faith Promise

Oswald J. Smith has been called the "father of the Faith Promise." But the development of Faith Promise as a specific way to give for missions has its roots more than 100 years ago in the work of A. B. Simpson, founder of the Christian and Missionary Alliance. Simpson's critics claimed he could raise more money for missions in ten days than they could in ten years. Later, Oswald Smith popularized the Faith Promise plan and used it to raise vast amounts of money for missions.

7. The Scriptural Basis For Faith Promise Giving

Those who oppose the Faith Promise plan of giving usually point to a lack of Scriptural references citing its use in the New Testament. While no specific reference to Faith Promise is contained in Scripture, the principle and pattern of Faith Promise are well documented.

8. The "Faith" in Faith Promise

Chuck Colson has said, "This is real faith: believing and acting obediently regardless of circumstances or contrary evidence. After all, if faith depended on visible evidence it wouldn't be faith." A Faith Promise is not made on visible evidence. A Faith Promise is promising God a certain amount of money regardless of circumstances or contrary evidence. The emphasis is on faith.

9. The "Promise" in Faith Promise

The principle of God's promise runs throughout Scripture. Joshua was able to conquer Canaan because God had promised it could be done.

Joshua saw the walls of Jericho tumble because God promised they would. Solomon built a Temple because God had promised it would be done. Jeremiah, knowing that Jerusalem would be destroyed by the Babylonians, nevertheless purchased land in the city based on God's promise that in the future it would flourish again. The writer of Hebrews summed it all up when he wrote, "For He who promised, is faithful." Faith Promises are made based on God's promise to enable His people to meet their commitments.

10. Everyone Benefits From Faith Promise

If so many of the churches who have large budgets for missions use the Faith Promise plan it must have some special positive benefits, not only for the church but also for individual members: world missions becomes more important and personal; everyone can participate; individuals grow spiritually; it provides opportunities to maintain a year-round missions emphasis.

11. Standard of Living or Standard of Giving?

According to Ron Blue, the biggest financial mistake his clients make is falling prey to a consumptive lifestyle. We are bombarded with advertisements to get us to want more, and spend more. The result is that most of us are in financial bondage that limits our giving. Freeing ourselves from a consumptive lifestyle will free up millions of dollars for the cause of missions.

12. Misconceptions About Faith Promise

As in every good plan or program there are always dangers to guard against. A Faith Promise is not a cure-all for an individual's or church's financial problems. Faith Promise can be used as a "cop-out" in giving. Faith Promise is not an excuse to start a business "to give all the profits to the Lord," expecting Him to bless it. Wrong motives for participating in the Faith Promise must be identified and avoided.

13. Beyond the Faith Promise

We need to be honest and realistic. Many people in our churches today have money. Whether through inheritance, hard work, wise investments, or a combination of these, individuals have accumulated significant sums of money. We thrill to hear how God supplied a $300 Faith Promise for a widow living on social security. But what of those who can write out a check for $300 or $3,000, and not even have to check their bank balance? How does the Faith Promise relate to these people?

Does it relate at all? For those blessed with substantial means, giving takes on another dimension.

Appendix A: How To Make A Faith Promise

How do you make a Faith Promise? Is there a formula to follow? As you read about Faith Promise or listen to it presented by a missions speaker, you discover there probably is not one "best" way to make a Faith Promise. But there are certain basic principles that should be recognized and followed in order for the Faith Promise to be understood and meaningful.

Appendix B: Most Asked Questions About Faith Promise

What do you do if the Faith Promise goal is not reached? If you are using the Faith Promise plan for the first time, how do you determine a figure for your budget? What do you do if your Faith Promise total exceeds your budgeted goal? Can a member designate where he wants his Faith Promise money used? Not everyone who has had experience with Faith Promise would answer these — and other — questions the same way. But there are some general answers that can provide guidelines to form a workable plan for you and your church.

Appendix C: How Faith Promise Worked for One Family

A personal testimony of the experience of one family that has been involved in Faith Promise giving for many years, showing the steps of obedience they had to take as they committed themselves to the amounts that God impressed upon them.

Appendix D: How Faith Promise Worked for One Pastor

The personal testimony of a pastor who introduced the Faith Promise plan in his church and the way God used it to help them increase their missions giving fourfold in five years, as well as increasing their general budget and paying for new buildings in the process.

Appendix E: Samples of Faith Promise Commitment Cards

Notes

Forward

"What have you tried lately that is working?" is a question often asked when people get together. We are constantly looking for new methods. In fact, it seems we have this insatiable desire to be constantly changing: trying anything new hoping it will increase our sales or output; trying the latest successful person's five point, sure fire, can't miss success formula; buying the latest management book in order to make us more efficient; trying the hot new investment model masterminded by a computer.

The Church has not escaped this appetite for change and upgrading either. You only need to go to your local Christian bookstore, or check the advertisements of any major Christian magazine, to see the latest "Christian" success formula or model being propagated by the latest successful pastor or Christian leader.

Missions has not escaped this movement either. Churches are constantly experimenting with missions programs and giving plans to see what will work best *this* year.

The Faith Promise principle of giving has been around for 2000 years, and used popularly for over 100 years. But we must honestly ask: "Has the Faith Promise principle, like other plans and models, had its day in the sun? Is it a method whose time has come–and gone? In this computerized, cellular phone age, does it work anymore?"

If it were just a method, perhaps so. If it were just a fund raising gimmick then it could be replaced. But it is neither of these.

It is a Faith commitment and therefore timeless, because faith is. Faith is part of the Christian life in every generation, every era. It does not get replaced with something different, something more effective or more efficient. Faith has been, is, and will always be, central to the Christian life. Therefore, it always will be part of God's plan.

Faith Promise, then, has not had its day in the sun. Its time has not come–and gone. It is still true that the great majority of churches who give large sums of money to missions use some form of the Faith Promise.

This book is designed to explain the simple "how" and "why" of Faith Promise giving and to give illustrations of pastors, churches, and individuals who are involved with it.

An Important note:

It is impossible to determine the total amount of money given to missions in the USA in a year. There are many ideas of what constitutes "missions", making the total different depending on your definition. For the purposes of this book we have used the figure ($2 billion) that is used often for cross-cultural mission work outside the USA.

About the Authors:

Keith E. Brown, has served as a missionary with OC International for over 35 years in the Philippines, Singapore, and Hong Kong, and has helped many local churches develop their missions programs.

John W. Hoover, is Vice President for International for Walk Thru the Bible Ministries, and has been involved in missions around the world for a number of years.

Other books by the same Authors:

It's Never Too Late To Say Yes
Missions in the Local Asian Church

1

It's All In How You See It

In a *Readers Digest* article entitled "Take Time to Laugh," a grandmother related an amusing experience. Her young grandson spent the night with her. At bedtime, he watched her putting on face cream and asked, "Grandma, why are you smearing that stuff all over your face?" "Well," she replied, "it's to get rid of my wrinkles." The little fellow looked at her, then at the jar, then back at her, shaking his head. "Grandma," he said gently, "it's not working."[1]

Wrinkles. Very few of us escape the inevitable lines that make ever-deepening creases in our foreheads and faces. In our search for that elusive "fountain of youth," how much do you think we Americans spend in one year to find it? Are you ready? **$500 million!** That's one-half billion dollars to reduce or remove wrinkles. Do these creams work? *Readers Digest* readers discovered the disappointing answer in the very next issue: "(Wrinkle creams) promise to prevent the effects of the aging process and to recreate the structure of young skin. These desires, which FDA investigators say lack substantial scientific evidence, have turned anti-aging preparations into the fastest growing segment of the skin care industry."[2]

Notice the word -- they "promise to prevent." Millions of people every year spend hard-earned money on wrinkle removers, based purely on a "promise" that these products will work. No evidence, just a promise. That requires some faith, wouldn't you agree? Interesting that many people who refuse to use the Faith Promise plan of giving, will plunk down good money in "good faith" with nothing more than an unfounded "promise" to cling to.

(Incidentally, $500 million is about one-fourth the total amount given by Americans for the cause of world missions all last year.)

Perspective is all-important. More times than I can possibly count, I have heard people say, "We really would like to give to missions. I know we should give some. At least a little. But you know how it is. There is always more **month** left over than **money**. We have house payments, car payments, plastic card payments, and after all, we have to eat and wear clothes. It all takes money." And the words flow on about how much they would **like** to give to missions, but just can't see their way clear right at this time. The conclusion: "We just don't have anything to give right now."

Is it really a question of not having any money to give? Or could the issue be something deeper?

According to a *Consumer Reports* survey of our fast food restaurant eating habits, only 2% of the people who responded said they had never eaten at a fast food restaurant.[3] (Never eaten at a fast food restaurant? Why, that's practically un-American!)

That means 98% of us have been there. I say "us" because I have been there in line myself many times.

When McDonalds added salads to their menu, says *Consumer Reports*, "they were so successful that they have appreciably increased the national demand for lettuce and farmers have had to plant more to keep up." Maybe that explains why the price of lettuce has been so high lately.

In 1993 (the last year for which data is available)
Americans spent $634 million for golfballs,
not to mention clubs, green fees, golf carts,
club memberships, etc. Just for golfballs.
(That's about 30% of what was given for missions)

What is the total amount of money we spend in one year at fast food restaurants? Hold your breath. $79 billion. That means, on average, each man, woman, and child in America spends about $170 a year for fast food. That means my wife and I spent about $340 last year on burgers, shakes, fries, and the like.

(Incidentally, $79 billion is about 40 times what Americans gave to missions last year.)

We **do** spend money for a lot of things, don't we. And many of them **are** necessary items. Take sunglasses, for example. I personally have received some "cute" remarks from my children about my sunglasses. (I admit my sunglasses are over 25 years old. And look like it. There is one compensation, however. They are back in style!) My eyes are blue. I **need** sunglasses. On the rare occasion when I forget to take them and the sun is bright, it is very difficult for me to see. I was shocked to read that we Americans purchase – brand new each year -- **90 million pairs of sunglasses.** Priced any recently? That figures out to over **$1 billion** a year for sunglasses.

(Incidentally, that's about one-half the total amount we Americans gave to missions last year.)

Recently it became "chic" again to wear the old-style canvas Converse basketball sneakers. When I was in my basketball playing heyday, you couldn't ask for anything better than a pair of canvas Converse shoes. Now, they are multi-colored. "Sneaker chic" they are called. To the tune of **95 million pairs** a year costing **$2 billion.** Two billion dollars – for sneakers that wear out in a matter of months.

(Indicentally, that's about the same amount that was given for all mission work, all over the world, all last year in America.)

How about soft drinks? Check the refrigerator or pantry. Have any in your home right now? I do. Being a missionary, I have been in areas of the world where a soft drink was about the only thing you could drink and be reasonably sure it was safe. How much do we spend for soft drinks each year? Over **$49 billion.** That's $200 for each person in the U.S. Let's see, that's $200 for me, and about $50 for my wife (she doesn't drink as many as I do), or about $250 for our family.

(Incidentally, that's more than 20 times the amount that was given to tell the world about Jesus who can quench a person's thirst eternally.)

Let's bring this food business inside our home. An article about peanut farming stated that the average American child by the time he has finished high school will have eaten 1,500 peanut butter and jelly sandwiches. (I'm sure I ate more than my fair share.) We in the U.S. eat more than 700 million pounds of peanut butter each year. Incredibly, that's enough peanut butter to cover the floor of the Grand Canyon. 700 million pounds of the stuff. Last night I checked the price of peanut butter -- about $2 a pound. That means we Americans spend **$1.4 billion** a year for peanut butter.

(Incidentally, that's almost as much as we gave to missions last year.)

And then, after eating all that good food at McDonalds, and gorging ourselves on those delicious peanut butter sandwiches, how much do you think we spend each year trying to get rid of those unwanted pounds we've gained? No less an authority than *Changing Times* reports that "people unhappy with their looks will spend more than $12 billion on weight-loss programs this year."

I know we get tired of hearing it, but it's still true. What other country of the world spends as much trying to lose weight as we do here in America? Think of it: **$12 billion** a year to lose unwanted pounds because we've enjoyed too much of our "blessings."

(Incidentally, that's about six times as much as we gave last year to take the Bread of Life to people all over the world.)

One of the things I enjoyed about growing up in West Virginia was going back into the hills at Christmastime and cutting a pine tree to decorate and display in our home. A big tree. Big enough to touch the ceiling. I was interested to read an article in the paper about Christmas trees. It said we spend about **$1 billion** a year for them. Not counting artificial trees, or lights, bulbs, bells, and tinsel.

And speaking of Christmas trees, what is the #1 item usually found **under** them? Right! Toys. Lots of toys. What parent (present company included) hasn't walked a child through the toy section of the store at Christmastime, struggling to explain to the child why she cannot have everything she sees. How much do well-meaning parents spend for toys in a year? About **$15 billion.**

(Incidentally, that's seven times as much as those well-meaning parents gave to missions.)

According to CBS News December 1994,
Americans bought 2.6 billion Christmas cards,
and 100 million Christmas trees.
About $2.5 billion.
(Given for missions: $2 billion)

Then there are pets. What would a home be without some kind of pet. We've had our share of fish and dogs, too. I don't know how much we spent for all of their pet food, but I did find an interesting statistic about cat food -- what one lady described as the "curse of the little round cans." How much do you suppose those furry little critters cost us each year for food (not to mention vet bills, grooming, and flea collars)? Around **$2 billion.**

(Incidentally, that's about as much for "little round cans" as we Americans gave to take the message of life around the world.)

Newspapers. I checked the subscription for the *Atlanta Journal and Constitution.* Fifty-two weeks will set you back $175. I enjoy reading the newspaper, and try to spend a few minutes with it each day. We also subscribe to several good magazines, including *Readers Digest, National Geographic,* and a weekly news magazine. Throw in *Ranger Rick* for the kids and *Sports Illustrated* for Dad, and a woman's magazine for Mom, and before you know it you've spent over $200 a year. Adding that to the newspaper subscription, we spend over $400 a year on "periodicals" (which by definition means they aren't intended to be around very long).

I began this chapter by quoting what I have grown weary of hearing: "We really would like to give something to missions, but we just don't have anything to give right now. Maybe next year . . ."

Let's get the big picture for a moment. For a typical family of four. (Dad, Mom, and two kids) who spend no more than the average amount for the various items we've just mentioned, what would the total be for the year?

Wrinkle cream	$8
Fast food restaurants	$800
Sunglasses	$80
Sneakers	$100
Christmas tree/decorations	$75
Toys (2 children)	$130
Periodicals	$400

TOTAL	$1,593

According to the latest statistics I could find, approximately 150 million people in American claim to be church members. About 90 million of those are church-goers, at least part of the time. Those 90 million gave approximately $2 billion to missions last year, or roughly $23 per person. (Let's see, that's about the price of a pair of sunglasses, or a small Christmas tree, or a subscription to a monthly magazine, or one trip to McDonalds for a family of five.)

If everyone who attends church gave to missions no more than they spent annually for wrinkle cream, fast foods, sunglasses, sneakers, Christmas trees, toys, and periodicals, that would be approximately $600. Multiply $600 by 90 million church-goers and the total comes to . . .

$54 billion.

(Incidentally, that's 27 times as much as we **did** give to missions last year.)

Perspective. I guess it's all in how you look at it. But it seems to me that obeying the Great Commission -- so that the whole world can hear the Good News about Jesus Christ -- is at least as important as the newspapers I read and throw away each day.

Realizing that over half the people in the world are starving to hear about the Bread of Life for the very first time, should challenge me to give at least as much to reach them as I spend each year at fast food restaurants.

Believing as I do that everyone has an eternal soul with an eternal destiny, should motivate me to give at least as much as I spend for toys at Christmas to tell others about God's original Christmas present -- His Son Jesus.

Missions experts are telling us that to complete the task of world evangelization -- "to the uttermost part" -- will require about 200,000 missionaries. To support those 200,000 missionaries would require roughly $7 billion a year. Add to that the cost of Bible translation, printing, radio, TV, medical ministries, literacy projects, and more, you are in the neighborhood of $10 billion. Every year. The question is: Does the church in America have enough resources to fund such a massive missions endeavor? Is it realistic to think that we can give $10 billion for missions, maintain our local church programs, and not die of starvation or go unclothed? Or are we too impoverished to do all of that?

Each day in the USA we eat 37 million hot dogs.
That means in a year we spend
$13.5 billion for hot dogs.
(About six times what we give to missions
in the same year.)
Hong Kong Standard, June 11, 1995

Let me ask you what I like to call the "$54 Billion Question": **Can we do less for the cause of Christ around the world than we do for ourselves?**

Robertson McQuilkin put the challenge to us like this: "Before the days of William Carey, the father of the modern Protestant missionary movement, the Moravians from Herrnhut considered a support of four people adequate to keep one missionary at the front. In such an atmosphere of spiritual vitality today, we would need less than 1 million Evangelicals to support all missionaries, and the Evangelicals in the small state of South Carolina could take care of evangelizing the world.

"But perhaps this is unrealistic. In World War II it was said that fifteen personnel were needed to keep one man at the front. If this same ratio proved true in 'spiritual warfare,' 3 million support troops should be adequate to support all the needed missionaries, and the Evangelicals of California could finish the task."[4]

I submit to you, it is not a question of what **CAN** we do. We have the resources.

The question, plain and simple, is what **WILL** we do?

2

Why Use Faith Promise?

On average, we Americans are generous people. We are usually the first to respond in any international crisis. Famine. Drought. Earthquake. Flood. Hurricane. You will seldom search long before spotting "U.S.A." on cartons of supplies sent to ease suffering and privation.

Perhaps nothing points up this responsive generosity better than what Ron Chapman did. Ron is a DJ (disk jockey) on a Dallas radio station. Having nothing better to do one day, he decided to try something different. Over the radio he made a simple request. "Go to your checkbooks right now! Write a check to 'Fun and Games.' Make it in the amount of $20 and mail it into this radio station."

In response, he received (hold your breath) **12,212 checks totalling $244,240.**

And what, you ask, was the charity or cause he was promoting? Nothing! Absolutely nothing. He never stated what he wanted the money for, or what he intended to do with it. "Just send it in," he told his listening audience. And send they did![1] (Ron later gave the money to charity.)

Oh, that we Christians were as spontaneous and generous when it comes to giving for missions. Sadly, I have been in churches where people would intentionally skip the service if they knew a missionary speaker or offering were on the program.

The Faith Promise commitment plan is used by thousands of churches to challenge and instruct their people in how to give generously to the cause of missions. It is not a gimmick. It is not a promotional fund-raising stunt. It is not a slick Madison Avenue high pressure ploy. Faith Promise is simply a plan God has blessed in many churches to implement His program for world evangelization, and to generate millions of dollars to support missions.

Is the Faith Promise plan the **best** plan to raise money for missions? Perhaps. But consider the following evidence that the Faith Promise plan deserves to be nominated as one of the most successful plans churches have utilized.

Suppose I came to your company or business and told you that I had a financial management system for you to consider, and told you that in a recent survey of the top twenty-three companies in American, **five** of them used this financial system. Would you be interested enough to try it? Probably not. Five out of twenty-three is not very conclusive.

Suppose I told you that in a recent survey, **ten** of the top twenty-three companies used this same financial system. Would you be inclined to at least seriously investigate it? I think you might because that means more than one-third of the top companies use this system.

Suppose I told you that in a recent survey, **fifteen** of the top twenty-three companies all used this system, would you sit up and take notice? I think you would. You might even be tempted to say, "I definitely will try it because more than half of the top companies use this system and if it has been successful for them, then there's a good chance it will work for me."

Of the top 23 missions-giving churches,
how many do you suppose use the Faith Promise
plan of giving to missions?
Not 5...or 10...or 15... but fully 20 of 23.

But suppose I came to you and said that in a recent survey, **twenty of the top twenty-three companies used this system**, what would you conclude? It seems to me you would be eager to try it. Why? Because it is a proven system used by more than 85% of the top companies.

Evangelical Missions Quarterly contains an article by James Reapsome entitled "What's Holding Up World Evangelization? The Church Itself."[2] In it Reapsome talks about the lack of prayer for missions in the church, the low priority missions receives in many churches, the fact that more volunteers are needed for missionary service, and the disturbing growth of complacency towards world missions.

He also talks about the need for money.

At the end of the article Reapsome asked Tom Telford, northeast regional director for the Advancing Churches in Missions Commitment (ACMC), to pick the "Top 20" missions churches in the United States, rated by the amount of money they give annually to missions. Reapsome admits that compiling a list like that runs the risk of leaving out many solid missions-minded churches. But the list will at least serve as an illustration.

Telford had difficulty limiting the list to 20, because several churches were similar. So it was expanded to 23. These churches are scattered all over the United States, and include various sizes and denominations, including non-denominational. Of the top 23 missions-giving churches, how many do you suppose use the Faith Promise plan of giving to missions? Not 5...or 10...or 15... but **fully 20 of 23**.

Several of these churches give in excess of $1 million dollars a year to missions. And the United States has no corner on such churches. People's Church of Toronto, Canada, currently gives in excess of $2 million dollars annually to missions, using the Faith Promise plan.

Suppose you ran an appliance business. Last year you rang up sales of $250,000. Down the street a few blocks was another appliance store. Both your store and your competitor's store handled essentially the same merchandise, brands, makes and models. Both stores were about the same size. Both drew from the same geographic area for potential customers. But you discovered that the other store had sales of $1 million last year. Would that make you curious?

There must be a reason for it, don't you think? If I were you, I would check things out rather carefully to see what the other store owner was doing differently. Perhaps he was marketing his appliances better. He might be selling them at more attractive price. His service department might be faster and more reliable. He might be advertising more, or staying open extra hours. But the point is, if it were my store I would want to know -- within the boundaries of ethical business practices -- what I could be doing to improve my store's performance.

Now, admittedly, that is a poor illustration. But I think it makes the point. If my church is giving a few hundred dollars a year to missions, and there are other churches of similar size and financial resources that are giving tens of thousands of dollars to missions, there must be a reason. They are doing something I'm not.

More times than not, that "something" is the Faith Promise plan. I have been a missionary now for 35 years. I serve with a non-denominational mission organization, which means I have to "raise" my own support. Because of that, I have spoken on missions in more churches than I can remember. (My record is speaking 25 times in one week.) Churches of all sizes -- from 50 members to several thousand. Churches of many denominations, or of no particular denomination. Churches in almost every state of the Union, and several foreign countries.

I have made one important observation. Almost without exception, the churches that are consistently giving significant amounts of money each year to missions use some form of the Faith Promise. (The word "significant" is significant. Just about every church gives something to missions. But if a church has 500 people attending on Sunday morning and a missions budget of $20,000 a year, I personally would not call that "significant." It's certainly better than nothing. But it's about one dollar a week

per person for missions. About the price of a cup of coffee. In my definition, that is not "significant.")

I am also in continual contact with other missionaries and mission
representatives. Their testimony is virtually unanimous. Almost without
exception, they have found that the churches who give the most for
missions use the Faith Promise plan of giving.

Several years ago Norm Lewis published the results of a survey he
conducted. He sent questionnaires to several hundred churches asking for
specific information about their involvement in giving to missions and
the use of the Faith Promise. Over 200 churches responded. Of those
responding churches, 179 said that they used some form of the Faith
Promise plan. Here are a few of their responses. (Answers were tabulated
in three categories: "yes," "no," and "no response.")

> Q: Has the Faith Promise resulted in increased missionary
> giving through your church?
> A: **93% said yes.**
> Q: Has it yielded a modest increase in giving each year?
> A: **82% said yes.**
> Q: Has your local budget suffered as a result of this plan?
> A: **92% said no.**
> Q: Has giving for local programs merely been maintained, or
> has it increased with the use of the Faith Promise plan?
> A: **83%** said it had **increased**.
> Q: Do you feel you would do a service to other churches to
> encourage them to adopt the Faith Promise plan?
> A: **96%** said **yes**.[3]

Although the survey was taken several years ago, it would be reasonable
to assume that similar positive responses would come if the survey were
repeated today. Lewis went on to make a strong recommendation from
his vast experience. "Literally scores of testimonies have come to me
through the years demonstrating the power of the Faith Promise plan to
produce money for missions. No other procedure can even approach the
results of the Faith Promise plan year after year. That statement cannot
be successfully contradicted."[4]

Pastor after pastor endorses the use of the Faith Promise and encourages its use by other churches. Consider just a few of their firsthand testimonies:

A pastor in Iowa had about 50 people on his membership roll, and a
$3,500 deficit in his budget offerings. The church was located in a small
town in the heart of the Midwest farm crisis country. Then the pastor and
his congregation discovered 2 Corinthians 8:1-5. They said, "Why should

the Macedonians have all the fun? Wouldn't it be an encouragement, a shot in the arm, a breath of fresh air, if the Lord gave us the vision to trust Him for a miracle beyond our ability!"

They began praying. At the close of their missions conference the pastor asked the people to consider making a Faith Promise. To make the situation even more unlikely, only two years before, the church had taken on a full-time pastor's salary for the first time, and miraculously had seen their local giving increase dramatically. Now they wondered if they could trust the Lord for more. At the close of the conference, Faith Promises totalling $5,030 had been received from those 50 or so members.

The pastor honestly said, "We didn't do it as giants of the faith, but more along the lines of fear and trembling. But we saw something in the Macedonians we wanted for ourselves and we stepped out." What has been the result? The little church has met its local obligations, the Faith Promise giving has been coming in, and the budget deficit that some thought would **deepen** has instead been completely **erased**.

From Indiana comes another example from a medium-sized church. Their first missions conference set a modest goal of $9,700 for their first Faith Promise commitment. When all the cards were totalled, $17,200 had actually been promised. Six years later, their Faith Promise had grown to $42,200 **promised** and $57,000 **received**. The pastor enthusiastically reports, "In addition to this growth in our missions giving, the average attendance has grown from 150 to 250, the local budget has doubled, and our members have made solid spiritual growth. Why? Faith Promise missions giving, plain and simple."

A church in Oregon shares similar excitement about their missions program and Faith Promise giving. During a recent ten-year growth period several things occurred. The membership more than doubled, and missions giving increased six-fold -- from $75,000 to over $400,000. All of this in spite of a recession that saw over 50 families in the church unemployed.

The pastor adds, "Some churches may fear that giving to missions will hurt the general fund budget. Not so! In these same years, we have seen a six-fold increase in total giving. **The Faith Promise missions program has not drained the church; it has ignited the church**. When a person learns that he can give abundantly to missions, he learns to trust God. When he learns to trust God, he no longer fears to give."

A doctor in Kentucky related this experience from his church. "Before our church became involved in missions using the Faith Promise, I used to go to the church board meetings and every month -- I mean **every** month -- the church budget would be short. Many months I would write out a personal check and quietly give it to the treasurer to help in balancing the budget.

"Then we began having a missions emphasis and began using the Faith Promise plan. A dramatic thing occurred. Within weeks, the local budget started balancing and in fact from that point on, there was always a surplus in the local budget, plus our missions budget increased each year.

"But then a sad thing happened. We got a new pastor who unfortunately was not concerned at all about missions. Before long we stopped our missions emphasis, and we also stopped our Faith Promise giving. And can you guess what happened next? It wasn't but a few months later that our local budget started being short again each month."

> *"My experience over fifty years*
> *of Faith Promise giving directly for*
> *missions has been*
> *that as our missionary budget rises,*
> *our local income increases."*
> **Dr. Paul Smith**

With all this evidence, why then do so many pastors and churches not adopt the Faith Promise plan? Several reasons come to mind:

1. It is estimated that less than 5% of all churches in the United States have any kind of active missions emphasis. That would mean, at a minimum, some type of annual missions event (conference, convention, seminar, etc.) coupled with a special giving emphasis to missions. Therefore, many churches aren't interested in the Faith Promise plan simply because they aren't interested in missions in the first place.

2. One of the biggest hurdles to overcome is anxiety on the part of the pastor. Many pastors honestly remark: "I know our giving to missions is small. We should give more. We would like to give more. But we are struggling to even cover our local expenses. If we start this Faith Promise thing and give more to missions, we will just go deeper in debt here locally in our church. People would be robbing the local budget to give to missions."

It is the unanimous testimony of hundreds of pastors who use the Faith Promise plan that such a fear is unfounded. Paul Smith, the late pastor of the Peoples Church in Toronto, provides one such testimony: "My experience over fifty years of Faith Promise giving directly for missions has been that as our missionary budget rises, our local income increases."[5] Rare is the church that suffers financially because it has used the Faith Promise plan.

3. Smaller churches read about larger churches with vast memberships and Faith Promise budgets to match. They conclude the Faith Promise can only work in large churches. Small church after small church successfully refutes that logic. I have been in many churches whose attendance was 100 or less, who still were able to have a successful missions giving program using the Faith Promise. As an example, First United Methodist Church in Alger, Ohio, has a membership of 100, and yet has a missions budget of over $45,000, using the Faith Promise plan.

4. Related to that is the notion that the Faith Promise only works in churches where the majority of the people are of above average income. Sometimes it is wrongly assumed that the reason a particular church always meets or exceeds its Faith Promise goal is because the missions treasurer has an understanding with a very wealthy person in the church. If the Faith Promise budget is short at the end of the year, that person simply makes up the difference!

Many churches of below average income still are able to use the Faith Promise. The presence of wealthy individuals in a church only means that the church's missions budget has the potential to be larger. But the presence (or lack) or wealthy donors in a church has absolutely nothing to do with whether the Faith Promise can be used successfully.

5. Some pastors do not feel any kind of special emphasis needs to be made for missions. They are not against missions *per se*; they just don't think a special point needs to be made about it, especially not a Faith Promise (which they sometimes consider unscriptural anyway). They believe if the Word is faithfully expounded, the members will naturally want to support missions in their own way. A worthy thought, but it just doesn't work in practice. You would hope that everyone in the church would be eager to support missions just because they knew about the Great Commission. But being all too human, most of us need some special motivation in this area, and the Faith Promise seems to help.

6. Some churches and individuals do not feel it is right to make a financial long-term commitment. I was talking one Sunday with a couple in California after a missions service in their church. The subject of Faith Promise came up. The husband said, "I just don't think it's right for me to make a commitment to a missionary saying I'll support him so much each month, because I'm not sure what's going to happen during the year. I don't believe it's valid to make that kind of commitment."

I asked them gently, "Do you make monthly and yearly commitments to other people?" Unless you're a very rare person, the answer has to be "Yes, I do." If you have a mortgage on your home, you have made a monthly commitment to the lending institution that holds the deed to your house. You have committed yourself to make a monthly payment. If you have a car loan, you have made a monthly commitment that you will give the finance company a certain amount of money. And all of us, whether we like it or not, make a weekly, monthly, or quarterly commitment to the Internal Revenue Service that we will give them so much money from each pay check. So we do make monthly commitments to give certain people certain amounts of money for various purposes. We should not object, then, to making some type of a faith commitment for missions.

7. Some churches hear about the Faith Promise plan, try it once, and drop the idea because "it just didn't work." There are usually several reasons why "it didn't work."

• The pastor or missions committee members, or both, are not convinced about it and committed to it. How often have you heard the truism "No stream can rise any higher than its source." The same principle applies here. If the pastor or missions committee members are not convinced the Faith Promise plan is valid and will work, they will not be committed to see it succeed. The pastor's leadership and support of the Faith Promise plan is essential to its success.

• There was a lack of adequate education and preparation of the congregation. Many churches make the mistake of reading or hearing about other churches who do use the Faith Promise plan, and conclude, "Let's give it a try." Then, without any preparation or education about the Faith Promise, the pastor stands on the designated Sunday and says something like this: "Well, folks, we're trying something new this year to help us raise more money for missions. It's called Faith Promise. A lot of churches use it and raise lots of money for missions. So we'll do it today. Somewhere there are some cards that you're supposed to fill out. Just take one, fill it out now, and drop it in the plate. Ushers, please come forward to receive the offering." The cards are then totalled up and the pastor and missions committee are disappointed at the poor response. They conclude, "Well, it might work in other churches, but not here."

I saw this graphically illustrated on two successive weekends when I spoke on missions and Faith Promise commitment in two different states. For both churches it was their first time to use the Faith Promise plan. The first church had about 125 people in attendance and received a Faith Promise totalling around $8,000. The second church had 1,000 in attendance and also received a Faith Promise totalling around $8,000. I used essentially the same message and presentation of the Faith Promise in both churches. Why the difference in response? Why did the smaller church receive the same amount as the church that was eight times larger? It's no great mystery. In the smaller church the pastor was totally committed to the Faith Promise plan and for several weeks prior to the conference had been educating his people in preparation for the Faith Promise offering. In the larger church, the pastor was not committed to it, did not fully support the idea, and had done practically nothing to educate and prepare the people. The results speak for themselves.

• The presentation was inadequate when the Faith Promise was received. It's not enough for the pastor, or whoever is receiving the Faith Promise, to say, "You have the card. Fill it out and we'll collect them now." The presentation and receiving of the Faith Promise cards must be carefully and clearly explained so there is no confusion about it. It must be explained so everyone knows exactly what to do and how.

Several things can be done to educate and prepare people for participating in the Faith Promise, especially if your church has never participated before.

1. Begin the education process months in advance.

2. The process must continue year round. Even in churches that have used the Faith Promise plan for years, a continuing education process must take place. New members may have no experience with Faith Promise and many older members may have never participated although they have heard about it many times before.

3. Use printed materials and books to educate the members. Have materials available in the church library. Prepare a special display of missions books.

4. Print information about Faith Promise in the bulletin for several weeks in advance of the missions event.

5. Have special bulletin inserts with Faith Promise information.

6. Put articles in your weekly or monthly church newsletter that is sent to all the members.

7. Have missionaries speak on giving through Faith Promise.

8. Invite pastors or laypeople from churches that use the Faith Promise plan to share their personal experience of how it works in their church.

9. Each Sunday school class should have at least one special presentation about Faith Promise. This could be done by the pastor, missions committee members, or by video.

10. The pastor or missions committee members can share briefly about Faith Promise in the Sunday worship services for several weeks leading up to the Faith Promise day.

11. Distribute the Faith Promise cards in advance so the people can be familiar with them.

12. The Sunday prior to receiving the Faith Promises, the pastor or missions chairperson should explain the card clearly to the people and urge them to be praying about their participation and the amount they will trust God to enable them to give during the next year.

13. New members classes should have a specific period devoted to your church's missions program, with a special explanation about Faith Promise.

A church in Moorestown, New Jersey designed an excellent Faith Promise education process for their people. Although they had given money for missions since the inception of the church, they felt their people could do much more and were convinced that the Faith Promise plan would enable them to accomplish that. Here are some of the things they did.

• The pastor and missions committee members studied and discussed Faith Promise for a year or more. They read all the literature they could find; they talked to pastors who used Faith Promise to get their suggestions; they corresponded with missionaries who were knowledgeable about Faith Promise; they attended a regional ACMC seminar to learn more. The leadership did an exceptional job of studying and educating themselves first, so they would be prepared to lead the congregation.

• The pastor and missions committee members started circulating materials and began talking to the congregation about Faith Promise.

• They set a time for their missions conference where they would receive the first Faith Promise.

• Four months before the missions conference, the church had a mini-weekend missions emphasis. Several things happened. A missionary met on Saturday morning with the pastoral staff and missions committee members for a question and answer time, all related to Faith Promise. A missionary spoke specifically on the Faith Promise plan in the Sunday morning worship service. A Sunday evening fellowship supper was held where a missionary shared again.

• Two months before the missions conference a pastor with 30 years' experience in leading churches in Faith Promise spoke at the Sunday worship services about how God had used the plan in his own churches as well as others.

• Finally came the missions conference where the Faith Promise was explained and received.

The whole process of education took over a year but the results were very significant as the church saw its missions giving more than double.

The evidence is overwhelming; the Faith Promise is not a gimmick for missions fund-raising, but rather a plan God has seen fit to bless in countless churches to implement His program for world evangelization, and to generate millions of dollars for the cause of missions.

3

Miracles Out Of The Blue

She was only a few weeks old in the Lord when she experienced an unusual and unexpected supply of her Faith Promise commitment.

My friend Chris leads a Bible study attended by this young Christian lady (let's call her Sue). A couple of weeks before the church's missions conference, Chris explained to the Bible study group about the Faith Promise plan of giving to missions, and encouraged each of the ladies to pray about her own commitment to missions.

One week before the conference, Sue called Chris and asked in an excited voice, "Explain to me again about this Faith Promise thing. I want to be sure I understand it."

Chris obliged, telling Sue how she should pray and ask God what her commitment should be, then faithfully trust God to enable her to meet it.

"Okay, great, I've got it!" Sue responded enthusiastically.

"You mean," asked Chris, "that you **understand** it?"

"Yes, I understand it, and I've got it!" Sue said with more excitement.

Chris tried one more time. "What do you mean -- 'I've **got** it'?"

Sue went on to explain how God had already supplied her Faith Promise in a most unexpected and unusual way. She had told God in prayer that she wanted to be faithful to give to missions what she should, and asked God to tell her how much that should be. As she continued to pray over a period of days, God impressed an amount on her heart. She prayed more, because she thought God must be making a big mistake. The amount was much more than she expected it to be. As she continued to ask the Lord, she could not shake her initial impression. She finally told the Lord she would commit herself by faith to that amount.

A few days later Sue's husband came home from work all excited. (You need to understand that while her husband was sympathetic to his wife's new Christian life, he was not yet a Christian himself.)

In his excitement he announced, "Guess what? My boss called me in today and apologetically told me that due to some computer mix-up I had not received the bonus at Christmas that was supposed to be coming to me. He was very sorry for the oversight, and handed me a check. Isn't that great?"

Sue looked at the check in amazement. "Honey," she began slowly, "You know at church we're going to have a missions conference in a few days. And they use something called Faith Promise to raise the funds for the missions budget. So I've been praying about being involved, and I made a Faith Promise." She paused. "I think this bonus you just received is to go for that."

Her sympathetic, loving husband responded, "Well, okay, if that's what you want. How much of it do you need?"

Her eyes met his, as she quietly said, "All of it."

It is the experience of pastors and missionaries
who have been involved with
Faith Promise for some time,
that God typically chooses one of three ways
to enable His people to meet their
Faith Promise commitments:
(1) Unusual or unexpected provision
(2) Controlled lifestyle and spending habits
(3) Creative strategies for generating income

The bonus check was for the exact amount of her Faith Promise.

Miraculous! Unexpected! Unusual! God seemingly dropped her Faith Promise "out of the blue!" That raises an interesting question: Is a miraculous provision like the one Sue experienced the **only** way God supplies what His people need to meet their Faith Promise?

When the Faith Promise plan is presented, a frequent area of misunderstanding occurs in response to the question, "How will God supply my Faith Promise?" Many times a particular Faith Promise experience is held up as the norm for all. If the Faith Promise is not properly explained and understood, false hopes and doubts may arise. At the end of the missions year, if God hasn't sent something "out of the blue," the entire Faith Promise approach may be brought into question, and people needlessly discouraged.

How **does** God supply a Faith Promise? How **does** God enable us to give "beyond that which we are able"?

Abraham's story gives us insight into the word "enable." "By faith Abraham, even though past age, was **enabled** to become a father" (Hebrews 11:11). God had promised Abraham a son. Abraham did not know how God would accomplish this, but in faith -- because God had promised -- Abraham trusted God and committed himself to God's plan. And the result? God "enabled" Abraham to become a father. The word means "to give the power or ability to do something." God gave Abraham the ability to become a father when his own natural ability was insufficient. In fact, non-existent.

The same principle applies to Faith Promise giving. God gives us the power or ability to meet our Faith Promise. God "enables" us to complete our commitment.

If we understand Faith Promise from the viewpoint that God "enables" us to give, then a lot of misunderstanding is cleared up. Because God is God, He can choose to "enable" me to meet my Faith Promise any way He chooses. Faith Promise, then, becomes something other than my sitting around with arms folded, waiting for God to drop something mysteriously "out of the blue."

THREE WAYS THAT GOD ENABLES

It is the experience of pastors and missionaries who have been involved with Faith Promise for some time, that God typically chooses one of three ways to enable His people to meet their Faith Promise commitments:

(1) Unusual or unexpected provision
(2) Controlled lifestyle and spending habits
(3) Creative strategies for generating income

The story of the "overdue bonus" at the beginning of this chapter is an example of the first way -- unusual, unexpected provision. Here are a few other illustrations.

My wife and I were in Lexington, Kentucky for a missions conference. I spoke on Sunday morning and closed the message with an explanation of the Faith Promise. The congregation was given time to pray and fill out their Faith Promise commitment cards.

Seated in the audience that morning was a man who owned a small construction business. He was very interested in missions and wanted to make a Faith Promise. But he had a typical problem -- no extra money. In fact, he owed $6,500 on a note at the bank that was due. As he prayed, he sensed God impressing upon him to make a Faith Promise commitment for $500. That was Sunday morning.

Three days later, Wednesday, he received a most interesting phone call. He had placed a bid on a job, and the owner of the company was calling to tell him his bid had been accepted -- with one change. He first must increase the bid by $7,000. That's right, **increase** the bid, not **decrease** it. The $7,000 increase enabled him to pay off his note to the bank, and his $500 Faith Promise commitment. Now, I think you'll agree that example falls in the category of "unusual and unexpected." Whoever heard of asking a contractor to **increase** his bid?

Here's the point. When this man filled out his Faith Promise commitment card on Sunday morning, he had no idea he would receive a phone call three days later that would supply the entire amount. But God did! As the man obeyed and stepped out in faith, God was free to provide in a most unusual and unexpected way, enabling him to meet his commitment.

A widow in Alabama was living on a small retirement. At the close of the missions conference she was convinced in her heart she should make a Faith Promise for $120. Considering her financial situation, that was a large step of faith!

During the year she received an unexpected letter from a man whose name she hardly recognized. And with the letter came a check. The letter related an incident that had occurred years earlier. The man writing the letter reminded her that when he was a boy, he had lived in her neighborhood. Though he was quite sure she would not remember his name, he was equally certain she would remember the time when someone threw a big rock through her living room picture window. That someone was him.

Recently, he had become a Christian, and in the process of confessing his sin, the Holy Spirit had brought to his mind the scene of a smashed window and a scared boy running away. He wanted to make restitution and had gone to a glass company to see what it would cost to replace her window as best he could remember it. Enclosed with the letter was a check for $150.

Unusual? To be sure! Unexpected? The woman couldn't have been more surprised. God had made it possible for her to meet her Faith Promise commitment – with a little something to spare!

One of my favorite illustrations comes from Dr. Paul Smith, the late pastor of the Peoples Church in Toronto, Ontario, one of the great missions giving churches in North America. Among the hundreds of people in their congregation who had made a Faith Promise was a young man who was a student in seminary, preparing for missions service. The amount of his commitment was $600.

A few days after the close of the missions conference, the young seminarian was having lunch with one of the businessmen in the church. The student was excitedly sharing about the challenge and blessing of the missions conference, and that he had made a Faith Promise of $600. At that point, the businessman became very upset.

"You're crazy," he shouted. "You're a student in seminary. I know you don't even have enough money to finish seminary. I know the financial struggle you've had. And now this! That Faith Promise will bother you all year as you worry about how you're going to pay it. That will actually hinder your studies. You're crazy!"

And with that, the businessman pulled out his checkbook, wrote out a check for $600, handed it to the seminary student, and said, "Here. Take this to the church and pay your Faith Promise so it won't be hanging over your head for the rest of the year."

Most unusual, wouldn't you say? Totally unexpected. Yet God used this unique way to enable the seminarian to meet his Faith Promise. Now, I'm not suggesting that when you make a Faith Promise, someone will take you out to lunch and give you a check for the full amount. But God reserves the right to use interesting, unique, unusual, and unexpected ways to enable you to meet your Faith Promise commitment.

After speaking at the closing session of a missions conference in Tennessee, I was approached by a man who sold medical supplies. He shared with me how God had enabled him to meet his $1,200 Faith Promise commitment -- a giant step of faith for him and his young family.

During the year nothing of any consequence happened financially. The family was having the usual assortment of problems paying their bills from month to month. Some time after the first of the year (and just a few weeks before the next missions conference) his boss called him into his office. The boss was very apologetic as he explained there had been an error in the accounting office and they had misfigured his sales commissions for the year. Concerned that he might have been **over**paid, you can imagine his relief when he heard that in fact he had been **under**paid by -- you guessed it -- **exactly $1,200**.

Unusual? Yes, because normally the accounting office was impeccable in its calculation of commissions. Unexpected? To be sure.

A lady in Atlanta saw God provide in a unique way. Two years earlier when she had moved into her new house, the man who helped her move commented that the Japanese maple tree in her yard was not only quite beautiful but extremely valuable. He added that if she ever decided to sell it, he would be happy to arrange the sale. At the time, she didn't give it a thought. After all, whoever heard of a "Used Tree" lot? She couldn't conceive of anyone wanting to buy her maple tree.

Now two years had passed, and the lady felt led of the Lord to make a Faith Promise commitment to her church. As she walked past her maple tree one day, the Lord brought that earlier conversation to her mind. She called the man, he came out, examined her tree, (now two years bigger and more beautiful than before) and took pictures. A few days later he returned and handed the lady a check for $2,100. In addition to buying her maple tree, he planted another smaller maple tree in its place.

Make no mistake about it. God does use "out of the blue," unusual, unexpected ways of enabling His obedient people to meet their Faith Promise commitments. I could fill many more pages with the stories I have uncovered, recounting God's infinite creativity in supplying what His people were willing to trust Him for.

I must admit, however, it used to bother me that I had never personally enjoyed one of those "unusual, unexpected, out of the blue" experiences in Faith Promise giving. It seemed that the only illustrations I ever heard when people presented the Faith Promise, were those exciting, often dramatic ways that God supplied the exact amount of the commitment. It bothered me that I had never received a dramatic Faith Promise answer to prayer of the miraculous kind.

However, that got me to thinking. Does God **always** drop unexpected, miraculous amounts of money into our hands which we then give to missions? (It had never happened to me that way.) Or are there other ways that God enables us to meet the Faith Promise commitments we make?

I started doing some thinking about how God had enabled our family to meet its Faith Promise commitments. Two other ways kept coming to mind. As I talked with others, and read widely on the subject, these two ways were confirmed in my thinking. We'll discuss them in the next chapters.

4

Lifestyle Giving

The second way that God enables us to meet out Faith Promise commitments is by helping us control our lifestyle, adjust our spending habits, and reduce our expenses.

God can choose to increase our income. That does happen sometimes. More than once I have heard people share how they had received a raise, for example, that was the exact amount of their Faith Promise. Sometimes God does increase our financial cash flow.

But we can also choose to decrease our spending -- by controlling our lifestyle, our spending habits, and our living expenses.

There is a term that financial planners use in helping people get out of the bondage of debt. It's called "delayed gratification," and it is diametrically opposed to what the world system teaches us. The world beckons, "You see something you like and you want it? No problem. Buy it. You don't have the money? No problem. Charge it, or borrow the money from the bank. Make small monthly payments and you'll never even miss the money. If you want it -- buy it now. Enjoy it. After all, you work hard for your money, so spend it."

There is lots of "gratification" in that system, but certainly no "delay."

Delayed gratification looks seriously at the choices and asks hard questions. Do I really need it? Or do I just want it?

Do I need it now? Can I wait another year to buy it?

Can I wait until it is on sale? Can I wait until I get my other bills paid and save up so I can pay cash for it? Am I willing to wait? Am I willing to do without it?

As we take a serious look at the Great Commission, and an honest look at the spiritual darkness all around us (over one-half the world's people still have never once had an opportunity to hear the gospel) we should have a different attitude toward our possessions, and our desire to accumulate things. In light of the staggering needs in the world, we should be willing to reorder the "purchase priorities" in our lives to free up more money for the church and its missions outreach.

Ron Blue is right. "The major key in reducing living expenses is recognizing that every dollar saved in the living expense category goes directly into the cash flow margin. Each living expense item must be evaluated item by item and then controlled. There is no magical way but each reduction frees dollars for other goods."[1]

I will admit that occasionally someone can take this principle a little too far. A newspaper in Oakland, California, ran a contest entitled. "How Cheap Are You?" to find out who was the biggest tightwad in the county. A retired welder who separates two-ply toilet paper to save one ply won top tightwad honors. "It's no trouble at all," he said. "It just takes a little practice." His single-ply rolls are "just as good as two-ply and save about 23 cents each," he added. He buys day-old baked goods and meats, generic groceries, and "whatever's on sale." He reuses plastic bags and never tosses out that final sliver of soap. "I've done everything there is to make or save a dollar. I'm not embarrassed at all."

The runners-up used other methods to save. A Berkeley couple said they save dental floss on a bathroom hook for reusing. Another man said he refroze used ice cubes. And one couple said they collected two-for-one coupons to restaurants, and then invited another couple. "We make them pay for their half and we dine free."

What can you do to control living expenses in order to free up dollars to channel toward your Faith Promise? Here are four target areas:

1. Reduce your living expenses.

This concept can be illustrated by the shopping we do for food and other items in the supermarket. How much do you spend at the supermarket each month? How much could you save with more carefully controlled shopping and spending? It's no secret that supermarkets try to do everything they can to coax you to shop longer so you'll spend more. The music, for example, is always soft, enjoyable, and pleasant to listen to. Purpose? To keep you in the store as long as possible. Jumpy, fast music would unconsciously speed you up. Moving a brand from the bottom shelf to eye level can increase sales by 50 percent. It's no surprise, then, that gourmet foods and high profit margin items are at eye level, while staples are down low.

In a test reported in *Consumer Reports*, identical shopping lists were given to two staff members, with instructions for one to shop quickly and choose items impulsively without comparing prices or brands, and the other to shop wisely and carefully. The shopper buying impulsively wound up spending $111.05. The careful shopper purchased the same items, but mostly store brands. She spent $59.35, a savings of $50.70 for the identical shopping list.

Careful, controlled shopping does not mean making do with inferior, lower quality products. It simply means shopping wisely, using coupons, shopping for specials, shopping consistently at the store that has the lowest prices. The article concluded by saying that shopping the way the careful shopper did, you would be able to save $2,500 a year buying for a family of four.[2]

And that's just in supermarkets. How much could you save (and in the process put extra money back in your pocket or purse for a Faith Promise) shopping wisely for other things? An article in the *Atlanta Journal*[3] illustrated what could happen by doing some wise comparison shopping. The buyer priced eight common items most families would have in their home (underwear, hair dryer, game, can opener, sauce pan, jeans, aftershave lotion, and picnic thermos) at the three largest discount stores in the same area. With wise comparison shopping on those same items you would save $30.56. When you begin multiplying that out over a year, you have saved a significant amount of money. Think how much more you could give to your church and missions if you made that one small change in your lifestyle and spending habits.

According to the most recent figures,
the average US consumer owes $3,300
in credit-card debt.
Assuming 17.7% annual interest charges,
how long would it take to pay off that balance
if you paid only the minimum monthly payment?
Four, Seven, Twelve, Nineteen years?
Answer: Nineteen years.

Here are some more practical examples of what others have done to help curb their living expenses.

• Brown-bag your lunch. Check it out yourself. Figuring a modest $4 a day for lunch out, in one week you have spent $20, and in a year $1,000. Suppose you brown-bag your lunch. It would cost about $1.50 a day, or $7.50 a week, or $375 a year. The difference is $625. Wouldn't that go a long way toward a Faith Promise commitment?

• Eliminate one slice of bread a day, and save $12 a year.

• Use powdered milk instead of regular milk, and cut your milk costs in half.

- Adjust your thermostat to 80 degrees in summer, 68 degrees in winter. It not only saves oil and gas, but puts extra money in your pocket for missions.
- Change your own oil, and save $15 every time you do.
- Pump your own gas, and save about 10 cents on every gallon.
- Wash your clothes in cold water instead of hot. Your clothes will be just as clean, and you will save about $15 a year.
- Take a shower instead of a tub bath, and save about $15 a year in hot water bills.
- Eliminate eating out one night a month.
- Cut costs on other purchases by merely comparison shopping and buying more wisely, waiting for items to go on sale, or postponing a purchase indefinitely.
- Ask friends for tips on how **they** keep expenses down.
- Don't automatically buy the top-of-the-line of anything, especially appliances, cars, and clothing.
- Shop the want ads, and clip and use coupons -- but only for items you have already decided to buy.

You might be tempted to say, "What difference does $15 make in the final analysis?" Obviously $15 is not much -- by itself. But the cumulative effect of making several small adjustments like that can be significant. In fact, if you would just take ten items in that list and total the potential savings, you would quickly accumulate hundreds of dollars in a year. Those small adjustments in reduced living expenses **can** make a significant difference when totaled together.

In addition to reducing your living expenses, there's a second target area for freeing up money for missions:

2. Control your spending habits.

A career secretary friend in California perfectly illustrates the challenge of gaining control over our spending habits, and the benefits that result when we do.

Like many others, Debbie (not her real name) was addicted to shopping and spending. Every day when she finished work, she would go to a mall or store and shop. Frequently she would end up buying something she liked and decided she "needed." Saturdays offered her many hours to pursue her shopping habit. Everything she bought was charged on a plastic card so she could make those easy, painless minimum payments each month. That way, her logic went, she could enjoy the things she purchased but it was only costing a few dollars each month. (Sound familiar?)

Two things happened, which are all too common. She found herself deeply in debt, and going deeper each month; and she stopped tithing. With so many monthly payments, there was never enough money. Yet she knew she should be giving her tithe and she also wanted to make a Faith Promise for missions. She was doing neither.

Feeling convicted about her shopping habit, she finally made the difficult choice to control her spending. To accomplish this, she took several steps. First, she cut up all her plastic cards. Next, she forced herself to go home after work rather than to a store. On the rare occasion when she did go to a mall, she disciplined herself to just look, but not buy. She made herself wait until she returned home to decide if she really needed the item or not. Usually by then the decision was no. As a result, she gradually got out of debt, she began tithing, and she was able to make and meet a Faith Promise commitment. How did this happen? She made the difficult choice to control her spending habits and was faithful to keep at it.

3. Adjust your lifestyle.

I had lunch one day with a young entrepreneur in North Carolina who was going through this process of reordering his priorities and simplifying his lifestyle. He was the typical young, aggressive, fast-rising, successful businessman. He had the nice home, the Mercedes automobile, and the other things that spell success in our society where seemingly everyone is trying to imitate the "lifestyles of the rich and famous."

Then he observed that the "really successful" people also had a yacht. He proceeded to buy one and park it at the marina. He told me with a hearty laugh about the first time he took it out. He went to the gas pump and asked the man to fill it up. When the meter showed $200 worth of fuel had been put in and it still wasn't full, he told the man that would probably be enough; he didn't plan to go very far anyhow. He was paying almost $4,000 a year just for the berth at the marina to park it. He also said during the time he had owned the boat he had actually taken it out only one time. But, as he said, "I had my yacht!"

Then he started seeing things from God's perspective. And he started seeing the staggering needs all around the world. So he started the process of altering his lifestyle and one of the first things to go was the yacht. Missions became his priority and a simplified lifestyle became the first step in this man obeying the Great Commission.

There are a few people who are so deeply committed to seeing the Great Commission fulfilled that they have chosen to simplify their lifestyle in a radical way. Recently I heard about three men who went into business together with the purpose of generating money for missions. They made a commitment to each other and to the Lord that they would live on a very modest income and give all the rest of their money to the Lord's work. They determined that modest income level by limiting themselves to the same salary as they would make if they were missionaries. Their business has prospered to such an extent that in one year they were able to give to missions over $2 million. How? By being willing to adjust their lifestyle to a very modest level, in order to have the joy of giving a higher percentage of their income to missions.

I had dinner one evening with a doctor friend of mine in Kentucky. He told me about his daughter who was a first-year pre-med student in a fine Southern school. He and his wife had recently visited their daughter, and in the process, met a nice young man she had been dating. He, too, was a child of a physician. His daughter said, "Daddy, my boyfriend's father drives a big Mercedes. You're a doctor, too. Why can't we have a big Mercedes?" His answer reflected the priorities of a person who has made difficult choices about his lifestyle. "Well," he said, "It's not a question of money. We could, if we chose, drive a Mercedes, too. But there are other things in life more important than that. We choose to use our money for the Lord and missions."

In this age, it is refreshing to meet people like that -- and there are many. People who have made difficult choices -- sometimes unpopular choices -- but who have, by controlling their lifestyle, freed up thousands of dollars for the cause of missions.

4. Make personal sacrifices.

Examples abound of people and churches who made the tough choice opting for **personal sacrifice** in order to free up extra money for missions.

A Presbyterian church in Wichita, Kansas, had plans to begin a half million dollar addition to the church. About that time a devasting earthquake rocked Guatemala. In response to this urgent need, the church voted to scale down its own building plans, spend less on in-house programs, and send $120,000 to help meet the need in Guatemala -- enough to rebuild twenty-six churches and twenty-eight homes for pastors. The people were saying, "We are willing to alter our plans and reset our priorities to help meet the needs of others who are more in need than we are." God delights in that kind of sacrifice.

A pastor speaking at a missions conference in Georgia closed with a challenge for simple living and sacrificial giving. After the service a lady came up to him, handed him an envelope, and told him to use it for missions. Inside the envelope was a diamond ring worth over $2,000.

The next Sunday in his own church, the pastor related the story of the diamond ring at both morning services. After the first service, a lady went home and brought back a fur coat to be sold and the money used for missions. After the second service, another lady brought a silver service set valued at $5,000, with instructions for it to be sold and "recirculated" for missions.

During a missions conference in Pennsylvania, the host pastor was moved to make a Faith Promise himself. Some time later, a special need was presented. Once again, the pastor felt he should make a financial commitment to help meet that need. At that point, though, he was stretched to the limit in his regular giving -- not to mention his Faith Promise commitment!

He was thinking about this special need one night as he was going through his evening routine of eating a big bowl of ice cream. He stopped between spoonfuls and calculated how much he spent in a year on the delicious ice cream that had become his nightly ritual. As a personal step of discipline, and with a willingness to make a personal sacrifice, he decided to stop eating ice cream and use that money to help meet the extra missions opportunity. He was willing to alter an enjoyable part of his lifestyle to free up more money for missions.

In Korea a few years back, my missionary brother-in-law, knowing of my interest in Faith Promise, invited me to meet a most remarkable lady named Pauline, who was a strong supporter of missions through Faith Promise. Pauline was traveling with a group from the United States, visiting mission fields and checking up on some of her eternal investments.

Thirty years before, she told me, she had heard Dick Hillis (founder of OC International) speak on missions at her church. He challenged her to begin supporting missions -- a challenge Pauline accepted by committing a modest $5 a month, or $60 a year, toward missions. Over the years Pauline has continued to give. Not just $60 a year, either. Her most recent Faith Promise was $3,600 for the year.

I asked her the same question you might have asked: "How are you able to do so much for missions?" "I really don't know how," she answered honestly. "I am a retired nurse. I don't know where the money comes from. I live on a modest retirement income. Each month I write my missions checks (she supports several missionaries), and after writing the checks I pray, 'Okay, Lord, You take care of me and stretch whatever is left.' And each month God does it." She went on to say she does her part as well with a little sacrificial living and giving, and wise shopping. "Before I buy anything, I ask myself, 'Do I really need this? Is this really necessary for me to have?' If it is, then I don't buy the most expensive things. I shop well and buy everything on sale."

By being willing to sacrifice, simplify, and control her lifestyle, Pauline has been enabled by God to give large amounts of money to missions out of a very modest income.

Jerry Ballard, former director of World Relief, related one of the most moving stories of sacrificial giving I have ever read.

Jerry was in Burkina Fasso (formerly Upper Volta) when it was in the grip of one of the worst famines of the decade. In a small mud-walled church, World Relief had set up an emergency food aid station to help the people with the famine. These suffering people gathered in their humble, dirt-floored church to sing and pray -- and to take an offering. They were concerned about the people in their own village, and others down the road who were even worse off than they were. And they wanted to help, though they themselves were on the brink of starvation.

As the offering time began, one man carried forward an egg -- one egg -- and placed it on the crude table in front of the church.

A few brought coins.

Some brought jars of millet.

One woman carried a live chicken -- one of the few left alive in the village.

Another brought some berries.

It was all they had. Food literally taken from their own tables, for those who were less fortunate than they.

But one woman brought an even more sacrificial gift -- a handful of leaves. She was so poor and broken that all she had was leaves off a tree. During the previous weeks, three of her children had died. She had absolutely nothing. Yet, as a compassionate Christian, her heart of love compelled her to help others, too. She picked some leaves from a scraggly tree in the village, and brought them as an offering to the Lord, in order to help someone else.

God can enable us to free up more money for the cause of world missions, if we are willing to make the difficult choices to control our spending, adjust our lifestyle, and make personal sacrifices.

Anyone **can** do it. I guess the unanswered question is -- **will** they?

5

Creative Giving

Just now, as I write these words, my wife has returned from a wedding shower for one of our young missionary friends soon to be married. She handed me something wrapped in tissue paper. It is a lovely hand-painted porcelain plate that the hostess for the shower had made. It is a beautiful plate that we will treasure for our home.

My wife told me our hostess friend has painted several of these plates to sell in a craft shop. She told my wife, "I'm praying that I'll be able to sell all the plates I've painted. I'm trying to help some close missionary friends get started in their ministry in Mexico. They have some special financial needs. I have committed myself to helping them as the Lord enables me."

A timely illustration of the third way God enables us to meet our Faith Promise commitments – by **creative things we can do to generate extra money for missions.**

The possibilities are virtually unlimited. Consider:

A pastor's daughter made a Faith Promise for $1,000. She got a job delivering newspapers on a paper route. After taking out her expenses, she had a little over $1,000 left at the end of the year, which she used to meet her Faith Promise.

A husband and wife team started a small part-time catering business. All the profits are used for their Faith Promise.

A thirteen-year-old girl made a Faith Promise for $120. Her grandmother taught her how to crochet. She started making bells to hang on Christmas trees. During the year she made enough bells to earn $120, which she used to meet the Faith Promise she had made.

A lady in California uses her baking skills to generate money for her Faith Promise. A bakery in a nearby town usually has big unbaked cinnamon rolls left over at the end of the day. She buys them for five cents each, takes them home, bakes them, adds lots of glaze, then takes them to places where employees love to have a delicious cinnamon roll for lunch or break. She sells them for 85 cents each, using the 80 cents profit from each roll to meet her Faith Promise. (Is that what they mean by "rolling in the dough?")

A salesman in Georgia made a Faith Promise for $1,000. After filling out the commitment card, he began asking himself and God how he was ever going to find $1,000. It was as if the Lord spoke to him directly: "How much do you spend for lunch each day?" The salesman answered the Lord, "About $4.00." The Lord seemed to continue, "Okay, and you have a little problem with being overweight, don't you? You've been trying unsuccessfully to lose 50 pounds. So I'm going to help you do both -- lose weight and meet your $1,000 Faith Promise. Skip lunch!" Which he did for the next year, paid his Faith Promise, and lost 50 pounds!

Brian, 8 years old, was sitting between his grandmother and mother Sunday morning at the close of their missions conference in Mississippi. His grandmother leaned over and asked him if he were going to make a Faith Promise. Brian decided he would, but wasn't sure how much to commit. His grandmother suggested that $1 a month -- $12 for the year -- would probably be a good place to start. Maybe he could do extra chores (they lived on a farm), mow the grass, save the money he received, and give it to missions. Brian, in an eight-year-old leap of faith, declared, "I'll make it $20 then!" And he did.

He got a big jar and labelled it "Faith Promise for Missions." All during the year whenever he received any money, either for work he did or gifts he received, he would put it in the jar. At the end of the year, when the missions conference rolled around again, Brian dumped all the money from the jar out on the table and counted it -- $20.75. His mother said, "Brian, isn't that great. The Lord has helped you gather $20 for your Faith Promise, and gave you 75 cents extra for yourself." Brian, with uncharacteristic generosity for an eight year old, replied, "I'll just give it all." And he did. The next year he doubled his Faith Promise to $40. (Well, after all, he was nine years old now, and in a higher income bracket!) God supplied the $40 as well.

A wife in Birmingham, Alabama, felt for the first time that she should make a separate Faith Promise. Normally, she and her husband made a joint commitment. But this year, she sensed that God was asking her to make a personal Faith Promise for $1,700! She gulped as she wrote the amount on her card, then began praying about how she would be able to meet that commitment.

Shortly afterwards, as she was thinking about her Faith Promise, the Lord reminded her of a hobby she enjoyed -- making ceramics for friends. Thinking about it, she decided to use the skill to help her with her Faith Promise. She had never sold the ceramics before, but without any advertising, in six short months, she had sold over $1,800 worth. She used a creative skill to generate money to meet her Faith Promise.

Perhaps my favorite illustration comes from Frank and Bervella, a delightful retired couple in their late seventies. The first year their small church in Pennsylvania adopted the Faith Promise plan of giving to missions, they decided to commit themselves to $200.

Living on a modest teacher's retirement, and having already committed their tithes and offerings to the church, they were not sure how they would be able to scare up $200 extra. But Frank had the proverbial green thumb. So they decided to raise and sell potted flowers, which they did, and with success. That year they were able to sell over $200 worth and meet their Faith Promise.

> *"Every skilled woman spun with her hands*
> *and brought what she had spun ...*
> *and all the women who were willing*
> *and had the skill spun the goat hair ...*
> *See the Lord has chosen Bezalel ...*
> *and he has filled him with the spirit of God,*
> *with skill, ability and knowledge*
> *in all kinds of crafts*
> *to make artistic designs for work in*
> *gold, silver and bronze...*
> *He has filled them with skill to do*
> *all kinds of work."*
> *(Exodus 35)*

The year I met them, their Faith Promise was $1,200. I was curious to see how they were managing in light of a fixed income and inflation. Frank smiled and said, "Follow me." We went outside in that beautiful autumn afternoon sun and he directed me to a berry patch. Not a particularly large one at that. As we walked along he said, "We raise strawberries and blueberries to sell for our Faith Promise." Looking at me with a twinkle in his eye, he asked, "By the way, do you know how many blueberries are in a quart?" I had to admit I didn't. "About 500," he said. "We pick them all by hand." He added that everyone who buys berries from them gets a personal testimony as to where the money is going. Sometimes, he told me, people will reach into their pocket or purse and give him extra for the berries. Imagine -- $1,200 worth of berries, generated by a man in his seventies, with a green thumb, and all for missions.

Creative giving is not a new concept. Recall Moses' instructions in Exodus 35 about building the Tabernacle. Twice Moses says, "Everyone who is willing" is to bring an offering to the Lord. This was to be a special offering in addition to their regular tithes.

Some very instructive verses are tucked into the middle of that chapter telling about the gold jewelry, animal skins, and fabric the people were bringing. "Every skilled woman **spun with her hands and brought what she had spun** ... and all the women who were willing **and had the skill** spun the goat hair" (verses 25,26). A few verses later it says, "See, the Lord has chosen Bezalel ... and he has filled him with the spirit of God, **with skill, ability and knowledge in all kinds of crafts ... to make artistic designs** for work in gold, silver and bronze .... He has **filled them with skill to do all kinds of work**" (verses 30,31,35).

True, Moses nowhere says this is a Faith Promise offering to the Lord to be used "to build a Tabernacle." But the **principle** of people using the creative skills God has given them to build His kingdom is definitely there.

Creative giving, therefore, is using the skills and abilities God has given us to help further His worldwide program.

Let's summarize. It is my experience, and that of many others, that God uses three ways to enable us to meet our Faith Promise commitments:

(1) Miraculous provision
(2) Simplified lifestyle
(3) Creative giving

But that raises an interesting and oft-asked question: "Where's the faith in all of that? I can accept the notion that God uses the miraculous, unusual, and unexpected to supply my Faith Promise. After all, He's a miracle-working God. But where's the miracle when you stop eating ice cream ... or plant a berry patch ... or make ceramic plates ... or give up your lunch hour and shed a few excess pounds in the process?"

Let me give you another perspective. For me personally, with my almost addictive love for ice cream, to stop eating that frozen concoction altogether (especially vanilla ice cream swimming in hot fudge sauce and pecans) would be a miracle of major proportions. For anyone who makes a major shift in their lifestyle, a miracle is required. We do not naturally and easily do those kinds of things. Particularly in this affluent, success-oriented, consumptive age in which we live.

For someone who has been in the habit of buying whatever he desires and charging it -- regardless of going deeper in debt -- for that person to cut up his plastic cards, stop buying things on a whim, and cut back his purchases by a thousand dollars a year, would require a supernatural miracle.

Just today in the mail came a letter from a close friend. She said, "Jim's life (not his real name) is still in turmoil, seemingly from extreme indebtedness. Not knowing the value of a dollar could keep him from any financial solution to his life. His relationship with the rest of the family is bad, mainly because of his misuse of money, and his imposition on other family members because of his excessive lifestyle." It would be a big miracle for Jim to change his life-time habits of indulgence that have put him in financial bondage. To break those habits and the control they exert over him, would require a major miracle.

But what about the berries and ceramics? Where is the faith involved there?

When Frank and his wife made a Faith Promise for $1,200 in **November**, did they know how well their berries would do in **April** and **June**? No. In faith, they said, "Lord, we believe this amount should be our Faith Promise for missions in the coming year. Now. Lord, we trust You to give us the physical strength (at age 79) to work the garden, plant, tend and harvest the berries for Your glory. And we trust You to give us a good harvest."

They had no control over whether their patch would yield a bumper crop of berries -- a few berries -- or no berries. God controls the rain, the sunshine, the growth patterns. By faith, they made the promise. By faith, they planted and worked and harvested the berries. God caused the increase.

The point is this: God is not limited. God can choose to enable me to meet my Faith Promise however He designs. Sometimes He may choose to drop it in my lap "out of the blue." Sometimes He may want me to put action to my faith.

In 2 Chronicles 20, Jehoshaphat was facing a "vast army." God sent His word of promise to the people through the prophet Jahaziel. "Do not be afraid. The battle is not yours, but God's. Take up your positions: stand firm and see the deliverance the Lord will give you." Remember what happened next? "As they began to sing and praise, the Lord set ambushes against the men and they were defeated." The enemy soldiers destroyed each other. What did the people do? Nothing! They stood firm and watched God work. And by faith, believing God would help them, they watched while God did the unusual, unexpected, miraculous.

How about Nehemiah? God told the people to rebuild the shattered walls of Jerusalem. What did the people do? Did they just stand in front of the rubble and say, "Okay, Lord, You promised the walls would be rebuilt. Perform a miracle and cause the stones to miraculously jump into place." No, far from it. Instead we read, "Half of the men did the work, while the other half were equipped with spears, shields, bows and armor.

Those who carried materials did their work with one hand and held a weapon in the other" (Nehemiah 4:16,17).

By faith they believed God's promise that He would enable them to rebuild the walls. And armed with that confidence, they rolled up their sleeves and went to work.

Jehoshaphat and Nehemiah -- same faith, same result, different method of God at work.

God is not limited to one way of doing things. He is an infinitely creative God. God enables us to meet our Faith Promise commitments in different ways at different times -- one year by means of a miracle, the next by means of a creative use of a skill or hobby or a lifestyle change.

Same great God at work in a myriad of creative ways.

6

History Of The Faith Promise

To say that the Faith Promise concept of giving to missions began in the 20th century is inaccurate -- by more than nineteen centuries! For although the Apostle Paul did not use the term "Faith Promise," he incorporated the principles embedded in the Faith Promise to help raise money for the church at Jerusalem.

The Faith Promise plan as we know it today was essentially defined and popularized within the last 100 years, principally by A. B. Simpson, founder of the Christian and Missionary Alliance.

Prior to the late 1800s, faith giving to missions was widespread. George Mueller cared for thousands of orphans over a span of 60 years, trusting God by faith to supply every need. Mueller kept detailed journals of his prayer needs and God's remarkable answers.

One day a reporter asked Mueller if he had ever prayed a prayer God did **not** answer. To which Mueller replied, "Never!" Then he added, "There is one prayer that is not answered ... yet. I have been praying for the salvation of the son of a friend. He is not saved yet. But he will be!" And he was. At Mueller's funeral.

J. Hudson Taylor is quoted as saying, "God's work, done in God's way, will never lack for God's support." That trusting faith led Taylor to begin his own missionary work in China under the banner of the China Inland Mission (today the Overseas Missionary Fellowship). Begun in faith, the CIM/OMF outreach has been sustained by faith, trusting God to supply every need.

The Faith Promise as a specific plan for missions giving was the creation of A. B. Simpson. Simpson's heart for missions shines brightly in the sermon he preached at the opening of the newly constructed Tabernacle he pastored in Louisville, Kentucky.

In making an appeal to his congregation to complete the funding for the beautiful new edifice, Simpson stated, "There are two things this church must be if it is to be blessed. One, it must be free, free of debt."

And second? "It must be unselfish and missionary. If this Tabernacle is not able to give up every year as much to the great cause of the conversion of the world as to is own support, it stands as a living embodiment of selfishness and will die of the chills."[1] Later, as his ministry expanded into New York City, Simpson wrote, "From the first, the highest aim of the Tabernacle has been to labor and pray to carry out the Great Commission."[2]

Simpson did more than preach about missions giving; he mobilized to promote the cause of missions. He helped found the Evangelical Missionary Alliance to fund and commission missionaries. One of the principles embodied in the Alliance's constitution states, "It will endeavor to educate Christians to systematic and generous giving for this greatest work of the Church of God."[3] In this statement can be found two seeds of the Faith Promise plan: "systematic" and "generous" giving.

> *"There are two things this church must be*
> *if it is to be blessed.*
> *One, it must be free, free of debt."*
> *And second? "It must be unselfish and missionary.*
> *If this Tabernacle is not able to give up every year*
> *as much to the great cause of the*
> *conversion of the world*
> *as to its own support,*
> *it stands as a living embodiment of selfishness*
> *and will die of the chills."*
> *A. B. Simpson*

In the 1880s, Simpson inaugurated a new kind of meeting which he called a "missionary convention." In addition to the usual Bible conference speakers, messages were given on the need for evangelizing the world, followed by appeals to raise the needed monies for such an evangelistic endeavor. Although many supported Simpson in these efforts, it seems many more opposed him -- particularly pastors and church leaders. Their criticism of these early missionary conventions was really a compliment and tribute to his effectiveness. "He could raise more missionary money in ten days than they could in ten years."[4]

In one sermon entitled "The Grace of Giving," Simpson set forth a seminal principle of missionary giving. A key passage for Simpson was 2 Corinthians 8:3, "They gave beyond their power," which he explained this way: "God wants you to go about your giving as you do your blessing -- in faith. They gave more than they were able to give just because it was a grace."

Simpson defined grace in this context as "what God can do, not what you can do." He went on to exhort his congregation, "Give, believing that He can supply even more than you can see of resources and ability. Believe that He can save for you, and enable you to do in this as in other things more than you could in yourself, even beyond your power."[5]

Some, of course, took exception to this new approach to giving by faith. In answer to their questions and concerns, Simpson replied, "We have some light here on pledging for missionary offerings. Have we scriptural warrant for making an estimate of what we will give in the coming year for the cause of missions? Or must it be just to give as we can and make no pledge? Is this pledging system scriptural?

"I am glad to tell you that I find it right here in my Bible, in the tenth verse of this chapter (2 Corinthians 8). Paul says, 'For this is expedient for you, who have begun before, not only to do, but also to be forward (eager, desiring, willing) a year ago.' Now then, by the help of God, honestly and honorably meet it. Again in the ninth chapter of 2 Corinthians verse 2, we read, 'For I know the forwardness of your mind, for which I boasted of you to them of Macedonia that Achaia was ready a year ago; and your zeal hath provoked every man.' You made your pledges in advance. You did it in meekness and gentleness of spirit and it went abroad through the churches. It reached Macedonia, and it inspired them to do likewise. It provoked very many of them, and it was a blessing even before a single cent was paid. The pledging was a blessing, and it was undoubtedly acceptable to God. God was pleased with your planning; God is still pleased when you come to give at such a time as this.

"Reviewing our mercies and blessings, looking out upon the world, desiring to form plans, we sit down together and say, God helping us we will endeavor to do so much for the spread of the Gospel this year. We do not pledge it as a promissory note. These pledges will never be called for by the treasurer. They will never be asked for by a dun. They are simply endeavors. They are just like what the Corinthians were forward to do."[6]

Several key phrases emerge from Simpson's words: "more than you can see of resources ... beyond your power ... making an estimate of what we will give in the coming year ... pledges in advance ... God was pleased with your planning ... God helping us we will endeavor to give for the spread of the Gospel." Here, in capsule form, is the heart of the Faith Promise plan.

If A. B. Simpson is acknowledged as the founder of the Faith Promise, then Oswald J. Smith must certainly be considered the one who first popularized it.

In the early 1920s, Smith was called to pastor an Alliance church in Toronto, Canada. His first Sunday proved as life-changing for the minister as it was for the congregation.

"I became pastor of a church that knew how to give in a way that I had never known," Smith recalls. "I commenced my pastorate on the first Sunday of January. The church was holding its Annual Missionary Convention. Now I knew nothing about a missionary convention. I had never seen one in all my life, so I just sat there on the platform and watched."[7]

What Smith saw that first Sunday revolutionized forever his ideas about raising money for missions. Indeed, missions became the heartbeat of his entire ministry. His church grew to become one of the leading missions-minded, missions-supporting, missions-sending congregations in North America -- a vision for world evangelization that has spanned more than six decades. At his retirement, Smith's church was committing more than $1 million to missions each year through the Faith Promise giving plan. Today, Peoples Church channels more than $2 million annually into the cause of world missions.

Oswald Smith's influence extended far beyond his own local church. Also catching Smith's vision was the Park Street Congregational Church in Boston -- a focal point for missions in the 1930s. Countless other churches soon adopted the Faith Promise strategy for missions funding. The post-World War II surge in missionary interest and outreach was in large measure made possible by the increased flow of support that came from individuals and churches mobilized for missions through the Faith Promise plan.

While A. B. Simpson used the word "pledge" -- the term still preferred by the Christian and Missionary Alliance at their missionary conventions -- Oswald Smith first popularized the use of the word "promise," which he felt more adequately defined the concept. "Pledge" to Smith connoted church budgets, canvassing committees, and dunning letters. "Promise" suggested a commitment between two parties -- the Provider (God) and the promiser. The person making the commitment was responsible to God for **giving** what had been promised, as God was faithful in **providing** what had been promised.

From the Apostle Paul, to George Mueller, to Hudson Taylor, to A. B. Simpson, to Oswald Smith, history is rich with the stories of those who dared to trust God for resources they could not see with human eyes. May their tribe increase.

7

The Scriptural Basis For Faith Promise

Those who subscribe to and use the Faith Promise plan of giving to missions do so for many reasons, not the least of which is because it works.

Those who oppose the Faith Promise plan often treat it like an unbiblical invention of the 20th century. "Show it to me in the Bible and then perhaps I'll consider it. But I certainly don't find it in **my** Bible."

True, there is no commandment in Scripture which says, "Remember the Faith Promise to keep it holy." Jesus is nowhere quoted as saying, "Go ye into all the world and make disciples of all nations -- and as you do, allow Me to provide the money you'll need to complete the task by means of the Faith Promise plan of giving."

But on the other hand, a surprising number of plans and programs commonly found in churches today are nowhere to be found *per se* in the Bible. Sunday school, youth fellowship, choir tours, women's missionary circle, mid-week prayer meetings -- you'll look in vain for any of these in the pages of the New Testament. But a remarkably high percentage of churches have embraced these programs. Why? Because they are not **un**biblical (i.e., forbidden in the Bible), and they work! If the Faith Promise is rejected outright because "it is not Scriptural," then logical consistency demands the elimination of a host of other beneficial programs as well.

The **principle** of meeting together to study the Bible is well documented in Scripture -- and indeed we are commanded not to forsake the assembling of ourselves together (Hebrews 11:25). But the **program** of Bible study known as Sunday school (or Vacation Bible School or Royal Ambassadors or Awana) is unknown in the Scriptures. While not stated as a direct command, we acknowledge the Scriptural **pattern** and **principle** that give us the basis for having Bible study programs as a regular part of church life.

In the same way, the **principle** and **pattern** for the Faith Promise are clearly taught in Scripture, even though the **program** as such is not to be found.

Others have argued that the Faith Promise cannot be accepted because it is based primarily upon a single passage of Scripture. Again, if we are to be consistent, we would have to eliminate some other very important teachings found only one place in the Bible, including the concept of being "born again" (John 3), and the "fruit of the Spirit" (Galatians 5), to name but two.

The foundational passage containing the pattern and principle for the Faith Promise is 2 Corinthians chapters 8 and 9, where the Apostle Paul holds up the church in Macedonia as an example of giving. Paul exhorts the Christians at Corinth to make good on their promised gifts to help the beleaguered brothers and sisters in Christ in the church at Jerusalem.

First, Paul explains what the right attitude of giving should be. He uses three expressions that define the Macedonian Christians' attitude toward giving: "their overflowing joy (verse 2) which "welled up in rich generosity" (verse 2) with the result that "they urgently pleaded with us for the privilege of sharing" (verse 4).

If suddenly in our churches
an epidemic of "Macedonian Giving Fever"
broke out,
and parishioners began pleading with their pastors
for the opportunity to give,
there might well be a rash of pastors dying
from heart failure.

The Macedonians did not look upon giving as a duty, or a necessity, or an obligation. Their attitude could easily have been, "Oh, no, another offering! Paul always seems to have his hand in our pockets and purses. Now he's appealing on behalf of some group we hardly know, with a need we can't possibly meet. Look at us -- we're poorer than they are! Why can't Paul just mind his own business ..."

My wife and I were in a church in Pennsylvania speaking on missions. After the service we overheard a lady in the congregation muttering to herself, "Ah, those missionaries! All they ever talk about is money, money, money! Why did the preacher invite them in the first place?"

Not so the believers in Macedonia. When Paul presented the need to them and gave them an opportunity to respond, he referred to their response as the "grace of giving." Four times Paul mentions the word "grace" in connection with their giving (8:1,6,7; 9:14) -- a grace they demonstrated by their attitude. Notice the words: not just "generous" but "rich generosity." Not just "joy" but "overflowing joy." In fact, their grace and generosity were overflowing in such a geyser that the Macedonian believers actually "pleaded (begged) Paul for the privilege of sharing."

We had better be careful here. If suddenly in our churches an epidemic of "Macedonian Giving Fever" broke out, and parishioners began pleading with their pastors for the opportunity to give, there might well be a rash of pastors dying from heart failure. It is doubtful the average pastor who ministers a lifetime even once hears words to this effect: "Pastor, I'm so happy and blessed in the Lord, I just can't contain myself anymore. Please, Pastor, tell me quickly where I can give away some of my possessions and money. If I don't learn about someone with a need I can help meet, I think I'm going to burst!"

Thankfully, there are still some "Macedonian Givers" in our churches today. But precious few of them possess the grace of giving that overflows in rich generosity, that begs and pleads for places to share their possessions and wealth. Let me challenge you to try an experiment for 30 days. Tell your pastor you want to become a "Macedonian Giver," and ask for some suggested ways to give away part of what God has bestowed upon you. (Caution: If you take the challenge, be sure you have access to a 911 emergency phone. Your pastor may need it!)

Giving should be joyous and generous.

Second, Paul describes how the Macedonians gave. They started by giving themselves, and only then did they give their substance.

Frankly, Paul himself was surprised at what he saw. "They did not do as we expected, but they gave themselves first to the Lord, and then to us in keeping with God's will" (2 Corinthians 8:5). Later, in chapter 12, Paul says a similar thing to the Corinthians -- "What I want is not your possessions -- but you" (12:14). The priority is crucial. First and foremost, God wants **you**. Not your money, not your investments, not your possessions. All God wants is all of you, for indeed, if He has you, He has all you possess. If God has you first, totally committed to Him, then your substance will follow.

H. T. Maclin, a long-time missionary to Zaire, once told about a harvest service of thanks held in one of the little African churches. The chapel was typical -- about 20 feet by 40 feet, dirt floor, mud walls with poles supporting a thatch roof, logs on the dirt floor serving as benches. Who would attend such a humble meeting place? Who indeed! The people packed the church and overflowed outside with dozens more standing all around. No one noticed or cared that the service lasted four hours. At the close, people started bringing in their harvest offerings, which would be used 100% for missions.

Some brought fruit, a few presented crushed corn meal, others came with baskets on their heads containing live chickens. One or two dragged a live pig down the dirt aisle. A couple carried in a live goat. When it seemed that everyone had brought his or her harvest offering forward, from the back of the simple chapel an old woman began to make her way forward. She was poor. Everyone knew that, and wondered what she could possibly bring as her harvest offering.

Her one hand was clenched tightly shut. As she got closer to the front, though, it became obvious that her hand was empty. Someone gently tried to stop her. "Old woman, why are you going up front? You don't have an offering to bring." But the old woman kept moving forward. When she got to the front, she turned around and faced the crowd of people. Lifting up her two empty hands toward heaven, she said very simply, "Lord, I bring myself."

That, said the Apostle Paul, was the most important -- and appropriate -- thing to do: give yourself first to the Lord.

But the Macedonians went on to give something more. They gave their substance, their money. Several times in the passage, Paul mentions their gift: "they gave **as much as they were able** (8:3); "for the privilege of **sharing**" (8:4); "you were the first to **give**" (8:10); "your **plenty** will supply what they need" (8:14); "you in Achaia were ready to **give**" (9:2); "For the **generous gift** you had promised" (9:5).

The Macedonians definitely caught the "giving fever," as evidenced by three tell-tale symptoms:

They gave sacrificially. Paul describes how their generous gift flowed "out of the most severe trial" (literally, "much trouble") in spite of "their extreme poverty (hard times)" (8:2). Paul does not specify what those trials were or what had caused the believers' deep poverty. But the point he makes very forcefully is that in spite of their troubles, they refused to use their own needs as an excuse for inactivity. The need in Jerusalem was great, and the Macedonians wanted to be part of the solution. They were willing to sacrifice and, if need be, go deeper into poverty themselves, if only they might be God's channel of blessing to others.

They gave "as much as they were able" (8:3). "They gave according to their ability." Some commentators suggest this meant they gave from their known sources of income. God expects His people to give a certain amount of money to support the work of the Lord. In the Old Testament the starting point was the tithe -- 10%. Regardless of whether God's expectation today is that His people give a tithe (or something more), the principle is clear: when a need exists, and God has made it possible for you to be part of the solution to that need, give as much as you are able.

They gave "even beyond their ability" (8:3). J. B. Phillips translates it "beyond their means." That is, they gave from unknown sources of money. They were willing to stretch themselves out in faith, trusting

God to enable them to give even more than what they were expected to give.

We give ourselves as well as our substance.

Third, Paul says the Macedonians were giving based upon a commitment they had made the year before. Paul had been in contact with the Corinthian church earlier to present them with the Jerusalem challenge, and secure from them a commitment of what they intended to do. Notice his frequent mention of **time** and **intent:**

"earlier (you) made a beginning" (8:6).

"last year you were the first not only to give but also to have the desire to do so" (8:10).

"now **finish** the work by the **completion** of it" (8:11).

"If the **willingness** is there" (8:12) (e.g., you had previously expressed a willingness to do something; are you still willing?).

"I know your **eagerness** to help (previously expressed)" (9:2).

"since **last year** you in Achaia were **ready** to give" (9:2).

"but that you may be **ready** (prepared) as I said you would be" (9:3) (e.g., last year you promised you would have some gifts, and I have told others that your gifts would be forthcoming).

"if I come and find you **unprepared**, I'll be ashamed" (9:4).

"finish the arrangements for the generous gift you had **promised"** (9:5).

"each man should give what he has **decided** in his heart to give" (9:7).

Each of these verses conveys the notion of predetermination, planning, and intent. Clearly there was a **plan**, and it involved both **faith** and a **promise**.

I seriously doubt whether Paul passed out Faith Promise cards or pre-printed envelopes for the people in Corinth to indicate what they expected to give toward the "Jerusalem Relief Fund" over the next 12 months. But it would not be taking liberties with the text to suggest that Paul previously ("last year") presented to the Corinthian church the need in Jerusalem; he had given them an opportunity to respond with some kind of a promised commitment of what they would do; and now it was time to send Titus and others to collect the gift from the people -- "the generous gift you promised."

Paul, of course, does not refer to this specifically as a "Faith Promise" from the Corinthian church. But the principle of **Faith** is certainly there -- "beyond their ability." And the notion of **Promise** is equally visible -- "last year you had a desire to give ... now finish the work by the completion of it."

Our giving should be both planned (promised) and by faith.

Fourth, Paul reminds the Corinthians of the harvest principle: "Whoever sows sparingly will also reap sparingly, and whoever sows generously will also reap generously" (9:6).

Think of it this way. Imagine that you can turn the clock back about 40 years. As you survey the landscape of small businesses in America, you discover a struggling new restaurant venture in Des Plaines, Illinois. Nothing spectacular. Just some hamburgers and milkshakes, cokes and fries. (Today you'd recognize it instantly by its prominent "golden arches.")

Now suppose in those early days someone had offered you an investment opportunity. "Why don't you buy some McDonalds stock?" You think to yourself, "Well, there's nothing extraordinary about this little company, so I'll just invest (sow) $100 (sparingly)." Your friend, on the other hand, smells a good thing in the making, and invests (sows) $5,000 (generously). Now, whose investment would be worth more today? Not hard to determine. It's the principle of the harvest at work: "sow a little, reap a little; sow a lot, reap a lot."

In 1959 if you had noticed
that every office was suddenly buying
copy machines,
and had invested $10,000 in Xerox,
in seven short years your investment
would have grown to $450,000.
Had your grandfather purchased 300 shares
of 3M in 1913 at just $1.00 a share,
by today that $300 would be worth over $8 million.
Sow sparingly, reap sparingly.
Sow generously, reap generously.

I grew up a city boy. But I have been around farms quite a bit in my adult years. While living in the Philippines, I often watched Filipinos planting rice. So I have observed the harvest principle in action. Suppose a farmer were to say during planting season, "I'm tired this week. I'm not going to plant (sow) any seed. I'll just hope and pray I get some kind of harvest in a few months." Would you care to make any predictions about the condition of his harvest? During the season of harvest he might as well go on vacation. Why? Because of the harvest principle -- "no sowing, no reaping."

Or suppose he said, "I'll only sow half as much seed this year, but I'll give it twice as much T.L.C. (tender loving care) as last year. Surely the rains will come, and we'll have plenty of sunshine. I'm confident I'll still have a bumper crop." Would he? Of course not! "Sow sparingly, reap sparingly" – it's the principle of the harvest.

A seed has built within it a God-given life system that is waiting to burst into fruitful productivity. If you cooperate with that built-in system, the inner dynamic is released. The result is a harvest in proportion to the seed sown. That's the harvest principle: the amount of seed you sow determines the size of harvest you reap. If you sow nothing, expect to harvest nothing. If you sow a little, expect to harvest little. If you sow generously, expect to harvest an abundance.

Jesus taught the sowing-reaping principle in a group of short parables and sayings recorded in the book of Luke. In chapter 6 and verse 38 Jesus said, "Give, and it will be given to you. A good measure, pressed down, shaken together and running over, will be poured into your lap." We like to quote that promise of blessing, don't we? "Amen, Lord. Let it run all over me! Pour it on, Lord, pour it on!" By that we usually mean material blessings. But the verse goes on to say, "For with the measure you use, it will be measured to you." That part tends to pinch in uncomfortable places.

We like the "pouring it on" and "running over" parts. We don't like the "measure you use" part. Because using it (particularly our material blessings) implies responsibility, obligation, obedience. Jesus is saying we are obliged to use what He has given us. We have a responsibility to put our material blessings into circulation. The harvest principle is clearly stated in the Living Bible paraphrase of Luke 6:38, "Whatever measure you use to give – large or small – will be used to measure what is given back to you."

The principle is clear and inviolable: Small deposit, small return. Large deposit, large return.

The wise author of Proverbs stated the harvest principle like this: "One man gives freely, yet gains even more; another withholds unduly (holds on too tightly), but comes to poverty. A generous man will prosper; he who refreshes others will himself be refreshed" (Proverbs 11:24,25).

Notice the phrases "gives freely ... generous man ... refreshes others." And what is the result of this type of giving? "Gains even more ... will prosper ... will himself be refreshed." It's the harvest principle – "sow generously, reap generously." Notice also the opposite: "withholds unduly." And the accompanying result? "Comes to poverty." The harvest principle at work again: "sow sparingly, reap sparingly."

Paul wants the Corinthians to remember this principle of the harvest as they prepare their gifts for the needs of the Jerusalem church. He is encouraging them to give as the Macedonians did – "beyond their ability" –

and watch the harvest principle go into action. A Faith Promise commitment stretches a person, and puts him or her in a position to see the harvest principle at work.

Paul puts the proper perspective on this principle in 2 Corinthians 9:10,11. "Now he who supplies seed to the sower and bread for food will also supply and increase your store of seed and will **enlarge the harvest of your righteousness.** You will be made rich in **every way** so that you can be generous on every occasion." The real harvest is spiritual -- "the harvest of your righteousness ... made rich in every way."

Paul nowhere in this passage promises you wealth if you are generous. He does not say: "If you give a generous gift to missions, God is obligated to bless your business or your personal income; and if you keep giving generously you'll become a millionaire." That is not the harvest principle. Paul indicates that the results of generous sowing will be primarily a "spiritual harvest of righteousness" in your life.

All the money in the world belongs to God in the first place. When I give a gift, I do not make God any richer. It makes me richer spiritually because of the realization that everything I have is His and that I am giving because I love Him and want to give. In so doing, I grow spiritually. Generous giving is one of the keys to growth in the Christian life. It should not be surprising, then, to learn that the more our spiritual harvest grows, the more generous we become ("so that you can be generous on every occasion") and the more eager we are to give ("beyond our ability") in faith.

Generous sowing results in generous reaping.

Fifth, Paul states the purpose of giving. It is for the glory and praise of God. Giving draws attention to the faithfulness and infinite resources of the One who is the Giver of every good and perfect gift. Notice Paul's frequent reference to this purpose:

"We carry the offering which we administer -- **in order to honor the Lord Himself**" (2 Corinthians 8:10).

"Your generosity **will result in thanksgiving to God**" (9:11).

"This service that you perform is ... **overflowing in many expressions of thanks to God**" (9:12).

"Because of the service by which you have proved yourselves, **men will praise God** for your obedience and for your generosity in sharing with them and with everyone else" (9:13).

The primary purpose for giving, Paul states, is to bring honor, glory, praise, and thanksgiving to the Lord. We are not to give in order to put any spotlight on ourselves. The Pharisees did that and the Lord chastised them for their attitude. The Lord takes great delight in seeing His children praise and honor Him. Paul reminds us that our joyous and generous giving results in much glory going to the Lord.

Two other ideas are included here as well: "show these men the proof of your love" (8:24); and "your enthusiasm has stirred most of them to action" (9:2). How often have you heard it said, "If I can do anything to help, just let me know." That's a polite thing to say, but both parties usually understand it to mean not to expect much (if anything) from one another. But when you put money into an envelope and mail it to a friend who is facing extra medical bills, you are showing your eagerness to help, not just talking about it. You have demonstrated your love in a tangible way. Faith that gets involved like that "supplies the needs of God's people."

Faith that gets involved like that stirs others to action as well. Faith encourages more faith. The Apostle John puts it this way: "Dear children, let us not love with words or tongue, but with actions and in truth." If that's not plain enough, John gets even more pointed in the next verse: "If anyone has material possessions and sees his brother in need, but has no pity on him, how can the love of God be in him?" (1 John 3:17,18).

Paul expressed this same idea in Romans, when he said "that you and I may be mutually encouraged by each other's faith" (Romans 1:12). **Your** experience of faith is a strong encouragement to **my** faith. When I hear how God has blessed **your** church, that encourages **my** church to stretch out in faith, too.

We give so **God** will be honored, not so **we** will be honored.

Sixth, Paul wraps it all up by reminding the Corinthians of God's promise. "And God is able to make all grace abound to you, so that in all things at all times, having all that you need, you will abound in every good work" (2 Corinthians 9:8).

Many developing nations of the world today are in serious financial trouble. Billions of dollars borrowed in an attempt to bolster local economies has only resulted in double- and triple-digit inflation. In the final analysis, no country's economy can be stronger than the total amount of reserves supporting it.

The same principle applies to God's economy. God has promised to provide on your behalf "in all things, at all times, having all you need." What is the condition of God's reserves? Three words tell all: **"God is able."** God's reserves are unlimited, boundless, infinite, immeasurable, and they will never be anything less than that for time and eternity.

Faith Promise giving is designed by God to be sacrificial ("as much as you are able") and faith-stretching ("beyond your ability"), causing you the giver to be in a position to draw upon all the resources of the God of heaven, "who is able to make all grace abound to you."

8

The "Faith" In Faith Promise

In 1973 a church on route 46 in Netcong, New Jersey, faced an insurmountable problem. They had just built a new sanctuary on their recently acquired eight-acre property, half of which was mountain and woods. They were told they would not be granted permanent occupancy until they had sufficient parking. Trouble was, 40 feet of sheer mountain rose abruptly at the back of the church, leaving insufficient space for the legally required parking spaces. The cost to remove the mountain was prohibitive.

One Sunday morning Pastor Ray Crawford reminded the congregation of Christ's promise, "If you have faith as small as a mustard seed, you can say to this mountain, 'Move from here to there' and it will move. Nothing will be impossible for you" (Matthew 17:20). Then he added, "If you believe that, come on Wednesday night to pray with me that God will move this mountain from the back of our church."

The morning after the prayer meeting, the phone rang. It was the telephone company. They were planning to erect a new building and needed fill dirt for a large swampy site. They had learned that the mountain in back of the church had the correct proportions of sand, clay, and rock for the required fill. Would the church be interested in selling their mountain? (Would they!)

Within a month the phone company had hauled away 40,000 cubic yards of fill dirt, for which they paid the church $5,400, not only removing the mountain but leveling the ground for the required three parking lots and preparing them for paving.[1]

In his book *Lord of the Impossible,* Lloyd Ogilvie asks a penetrating question about faith: "What are you attempting that you cannot accomplish without an intervention from the Lord?" He went on to say, "Most of us live our lives within the narrow limits of what we can do in our own strength and talents. We keep life carefully constricted inside the boundaries of what we are sure we can handle by ourselves. In reality we don't need

God. Our fear of risks keeps us away from anything we cannot control or do with our own ability. Our vision of what can happen is usually calculated on what we are able to do with our own resources and experience."[2]

Ralph Winter's name is well known in mission circles. From his fertile mind have come a wealth of new tools and strategies in the task of analyzing and evangelizing the unreached peoples of the world.

One of Winter's major undertakings has been the development of the U.S. Center for World Mission in Pasadena, California. In 1975 Winter saw an opportunity for a strategic purchase -- not just a building, but an entire college campus. The goal: to bring together scores of mission groups working in cooperation to reach the frontier areas of the world, where billions still waited to hear the gospel for the first time.

Winter had no money. No funding organization backed him. No foundation guaranteed him support. All he had was a dream of what needed to be done -- and the faith to believe that $15 million was not too much to ask of God.

Winter has been asked many times how he could possibly attempt something that, humanly speaking, appeared doomed from the start. His answer gives us a good working definition of faith.

You cannot discover new oceans
unless you have the courage
to lose sight of the shore.

"When my wife and I made the decision (to leave the School of World Missions at Fuller Seminary) and walk into a situation which was itself ridiculously unlikely, we didn't do this because we had some scheme so we could see our way clear. But read Hebrews 11. **Faith is not what protects you. Faith is what guides you.** If I were to say that I knew this Center would definitely succeed, it would be nuts. I'm not sure it will succeed. I only know it is worth trying. Risks are not to be evaluated in terms of the probability of success, but in terms of the value of the goal."[3]

Chuck Colson, in his book *Loving God,* provides another operational definition for faith. "This is real faith: believing and acting obediently regardless of circumstances or contrary evidence. After all, if faith depended on visible evidence, it wouldn't be faith."[4]

A Faith Promise is not made on visible evidence. That is a pledge. When you make a pledge to your church, all you need is a calculator. "What is my income going to be this year? What is 10% -- or whatever percent you may choose – of that amount? That will be my pledge." There is not much faith involved. Just arithmetic.

A Faith Promise is different. It is promising God a certain amount of money regardless of circumstances or contrary evidence. The emphasis here is on faith. "And what is faith? Faith gives substance to our hopes, and makes us certain of realities we do not see" (Hebrews 11:1, NEB).

Bob Pierce, founder and first president of World Vision, had an interesting way of defining faith. He often used the expression "God Room." He explained it like this: "Nothing is a miracle until it reaches that area where the very utmost that human effort can do is not enough, and God moves in to fill that space between what is possible and what He wants done that is impossible. That is God Room." Pierce went on to say, "No faith has been exercised until you have promised more than it is possible for you to give. Without the miracle quality, you can get your life and business down to where you don't need God. You can operate exactly like IBM or Sears or General Motors. But the blessing will all be gone."[5]

Oswald Chambers captured the idea of faith succinctly when he said, "Faith gives God His opportunity to work. **Faith, by its very nature, must be tried before the reality of faith is actual.**"[6]

James expressed that same truth when he wrote, "You see that (Abraham's) faith and his actions were working together, and **his faith was made complete by what he did** (James 2:22).

When the disciples looked out over 5,000 famished men that day near the Sea of Galilee, their "God Room" was sadly lacking. Jesus first asked Philip, "Where shall we buy bread for these people to eat?" (John 6:5). Philip, looking through his natural eyes and seeing only an insurmountable mountain, commented, "Lord, it would take almost a year's salary to feed this crowd." What was he really saying? "Lord, it's hopeless!"

Then Andrew appeared. Apparently he had been talking to some of the crowd and had encountered a tiny lad with a tiny lunch to match. Andrew said, "Here is a boy with five small barley loaves and two small fish." That was a statement of faith. He should have stopped there. But he went on, "BUT – how far will they go among so many?" (John 6:8,9).

Andrew's problem – which is too often our problem – was simply that he was trying to stretch human resources to meet superhuman demands. He hadn't considered his "God Room." Neither he nor any of the disciples had taken into account the greatest resource they had – the Lord Jesus. After all, who had created the fish and grain in the first place? As the disciples looked at the impossible problem they faced, they were tempted to conclude that the demand outweighed the supply, and therefore the situation was hopeless.

In the wealthier sections of many cities and towns today, you will observe homes surrounded by walls, often eight to ten feet high and one to three feet thick. These walls provide reasonable protection and security from thieves and unwanted intruders.

By contrast, the walls of Jericho were in another league altogether. Archaeologists estimate from the rubble that the walls stood taller than a five-story building, and were thick enough for city dwellers to build their homes inside. In a word, an **impossible** obstacle for an advancing army. (And especially one lacking in chariots, artillery, explosives, and high-powered wall whackers.)

Armed with nothing more potent than faith in God, General Joshua did the only thing left to do: he obeyed God. And the result was a victory only faith could provide.

When we have faith in God, we discover God often uses unorthodox, unusual, and even inexplicable methods (humanly speaking) to accomplish His will. Suppose you had been Joshua. You knew you had to take the walled city of Jericho and defeat the enemy. The Lord appears to you and gives you His plan of attack. Faith required? You'd better believe it!

Then as commander of the troops, it is your job to give the battlefield instructions to your platoon leaders.

"How are we going to defeat the enemy and take the city, Joshua, sir?"

"Well -- er -- ahh -- men, here is our battle plan. Remember now, this plan came from the Lord. We're going to get the Ark of the Covenant, then we'll all fall in behind it, with the priests out in front. Then for six days we'll walk around the walls once each day. No one is to say a word. And then, on the seventh day, we'll walk around the wall seven times and when I give the order, we'll all shout real loud and -- boom -- just like that the walls will collapse and the city will be ours."

Simple? Yes. Doable? To be sure. Believable? Not very.

But according to the record in Joshua 6 not one person snickered or questioned, objected or doubted. In obedience, they followed the Lord and Joshua, and the rest is military history.

Faith Promise giving is something like that. As we prayerfully, obediently look to God, asking what He would have us do for our Faith Promise, it might look to our human eyes like a totally hopeless, impossible situation. And we are tempted to say, "Lord, You've got to be kidding!!" And we might be tempted to add, "By faith, Lord? That's too unorthodox. That's too unusual. Why, Lord, that's just completely crazy."

Faith says: "Lord, it looks impossible to me. But help me to see this through Your eyes of faith and be willing to trust You to do what only You can do through my obedience."

Earlier in the book of Numbers, Moses faced another of those impossible situations while preparing to enter the Promised Land. On instructions from the Lord, Moses sent out twelve men to do a reconnaissance mission in the land of Canaan. They were to spy out the enemies' fortifications and the condition of the land, and bring back a report to Moses. Ten submitted the "majority report" which went something like this: "The people are powerful and about nine feet tall. The cities are fortified and very large. They have big thick walls, which are very high, and the surrounding cities are filled with many people (reinforcements)." In a word, the enemy is too big, too strong, and too numerous!

Their conclusion: MISSION IMPOSSIBLE.

Interestingly, they had also observed that the land was flowing with milk and honey and was filled with delicious fruit. In fact, they brought back with them Exhibit A of the fruit – an enormous cluster of prize-winning grapes. I like grapes. When I go to the supermarket I can carry several clusters of grapes in the palm of my hand. But they had to put Exhibit A on a pole and have two men carry it on their shoulders. And that was just **one** cluster of grapes. In spite of the bounty in the land, their conclusion was unwavering: IT'S IMPOSSIBLE. To them, the equation looked like this:

$$\textbf{\textit{Walls + Giants - Faith = Impossibility}}$$

But there was also a "minority report." It is interesting to note that all twelve spies saw exactly the same thing. The two in the minority, Caleb and Joshua, saw the same walls, the same giants, the same fortified cities. But they saw something more. They saw God. Their report was a faith-inspired report, "Yes, it's true. There are high walls and they are thick. There are giants in the land and they are many. Compared to them we look like grasshoppers. And there are many 'reinforcements' in the cities nearby that we will have to neutralize as well. But nonetheless we should go up and take possession of the land. WE CAN CERTAINLY DO IT." To their way of thinking, the equation read:

$$\textbf{\textit{Walls + Giants + Faith = Assured Victory}}$$

Faith Promises are made with that same trusting belief in the Lord. The dollar amount of my commitment may loom large – much bigger than I could ever expect to give, humanly speaking. But I also see God in the equation, and in faith I stretch myself to trust Him that He will enable me to meet the goal I believe He has led me to make.

David had faith like that when he went out to face a giant-sized foe named Goliath. No one from Israel's vast army had dared to face Goliath in battle, and small wonder. Measuring more than nine feet tall, wearing a coat of armor that weighed 125 pounds, and carrying a spear whose tip alone weighed 15 pounds, he was a terrifying sight. For days Goliath had publicly denounced the Israelites, mocking their cowardice, and casting ridicule upon their God.

Let's be honest. We would have been hiding behind our tent flaps, too. And apparently the rest of the army had been staying out of sight. One word amply describes the scene -- IMPOSSIBLE. "When the Israelites saw (Goliath), they all ran from him in great fear" (1 Samuel 17:24). They saw the size of the enemy -- instead of the size of their God. They had great fear -- instead of great faith. And the predictable result? They all ran.

> *You can't get to second base*
> *if you keep your foot on first.*

The principle for us is clear: If you focus on the foe, inevitably you will become fearful and run. If you focus on God, inevitably you will have faith and win. The same principle holds true with the Faith Promise. If you only focus on the amount God wants you to give, and your own resources limited as they are, then you will not stretch yourself out on God by faith. Your only conclusion will be -- IT'S IMPOSSIBLE.

But if you see the amount God wants you to give, regardless of your present resources or circumstances, and then add faith to the equation, you will stretch yourself out on God and conclude -- MISSION POSSIBLE. It's not great faith in God that enables you to do great things, but rather faith in a great God.

A teenager's example of trusting faith provides a beautiful story to conclude this chapter. *Guidepost* magazine carried the story of one family's experience in seeing God provide for them in an impossible situation.

"At one point during the winter of 1940, my husband, a house painter, was temporarily unemployed because of the weather, and the textile plant where I worked was closed due to a seasonal lay-off. We literally had no money. To make matters worse, our 18 month old daughter, Rachel, was recovering poorly from pneumonia, and the doctor insisted we feed her a boiled egg each day. Even that was beyond our means.

"'Why not pray for an egg?' suggested our baby-sitter, who was staying on without pay to help us. We were a churchgoing family, but this teenager's depth of faith was something new to us at the time. All the same, she and I got on our knees and told the Lord that Rachel needed an egg each morning. We left the problem in His hands.

"About 10 o'clock that morning we heard some cackling coming from the hedge fence in front of our house. There among the bare branches sat a fat red hen. We had no idea where she had come from. We just watched in amazement as she laid one egg and then proceeded down the road, out of sight.

"The little red hen that first day was a surprise, and we thanked God for it, but can you imagine how startled we were when we heard the hen cackling in the hedge the next morning? And the morning after that, and the morning after that? Every day for over a week, Rachel had a fresh boiled egg.

"Rachel grew better and better, and at last the weather turned and my husband went back to work. The next morning I waited by the window and watched. But our prayers had been answered -- precisely.

"That little red hen did not come back. Ever."[7]

Moral of the story: Faith must be **enjoined** before its reality can be **enjoyed**.

9

The "Promise" In Faith Promise

As General Joshua assumed the reins of leadership in the Hebrew nation after the death of Moses, God came to him with specific instructions. God reminded Joshua to be strong and courageous, to follow all the commandments contained in the law, to meditate upon that law day and night. God assured Joshua of His abiding presence and help in conquering the Promised Land. Comforting words for a new Administration.

God began the conversation with a promise: "I will give you every place where you set your foot as I promised Moses" (Joshua 1:3). Later on, as Joshua recounted these events, he made a bold statement: "Not one of all the Lord's good promises to the house of Israel failed; every one was fulfilled" (21:45). Still later, as Joshua sensed that his life on earth was coming to an end, he reiterated his total faith in God and the reason he could trust like he did: "Now I am about to go the way of all earth. You know with all your heart and soul that not one of all the good promises the Lord your God gave you has failed. Every promise has been fulfilled; not one has failed" (23:14).

Centuries later in Israel's history, King Solomon reminded the people of the same truth. In his prayer at the dedication of the Temple, Solomon acknowledged God's faithfulness. "You have kept your promise to your servant David my father; with your mouth you have promised and with your hand you have fulfilled it as it is today." After Solomon had finished his prayers and supplications to the Lord, he stood and blessed the whole congregation. Again he reminded the people of God's faithfulness. "Praise be to the Lord, who has given rest to his people Israel just as he promised. Not one word has failed of all the good promises he gave through his servant Moses" (1 Kings 8:24,56).

The principle set forth in these verses is eloquent in its simplicity: **God faithfully fulfills His promises**. It's a theme that permeates and saturates the Scriptures. God's promises are trustworthy "for he who promised is faithful" (Hebrews 10:23).

Faith in God is never misplaced. And a Faith Promise is simply promising in **faith** what God has promised in **fact**. When I make a Faith Promise commitment I cannot see at that moment how God will enable me to fulfill it. But as I exercise my faith in God, based on His promise to supply, I can start looking expectantly for ways (often unexpected) in which God will enable me to meet my commitment.

We see this principle at work in the national life of Israel. "The Lord said to Moses, Command the Israelites and say to them: When you enter Canaan. . ." (Numbers 34:11). What follows is a detailed description of the twelve tribes' inheritance in the land of Canaan. The important word is **when:** "When you enter Canaan." They were not there yet. They really didn't know at that point how it was all going to happen. But God promised them thousands of square miles of real estate -- by faith -- when as yet the nation of Israel did not possess so much as a spade full.

Representatives from each of the twelve tribes selected their respective portion of the Promise Land -- by faith -- even before they had set foot in their new "homeland." The Levites were given 48 cities -- by faith -- not one of which had yet been conquered. By faith -- based on God's promise alone -- they engaged the enemy and began fighting **battles which had already been won, even though they had yet to be fought.**

God repeated this principle to Moses when He said, "For you **will bring** (notice the future tense) the Israelites into the land I **promised** them (notice the past tense) and I myself will be with you" (Deuteronomy 31:23).

The city of Jericho loomed like a taunting sentinel -- a seemingly impossible obstacle in the path of Joshua's dreams of conquest. But Joshua possessed one "secret weapon" his enemies lacked: the promise of God. "Then the Lord said to Joshua, See, I have delivered Jericho into your hands" (Joshua 6:2). God wanted Joshua to see what only the eyes of faith can observe.

Had Joshua and his army already achieved victory over Jericho? Had the enemy inhabitants of Canaan already capitulated? Had Jericho's massive walls already crumbled and collapsed? **In fact**, no. Yet, God promised certain victory. Fortified with that promise, **in faith**, the people proceeded with God's plan. In obedience to God, based on His promise alone, they moved out and conquered. God did not explain to them how it was all going to happen (it's doubtful they would have believed Him if He had). God simply promised that Jericho's mighty walls would fall -- by faith.

A Faith Promise is like that. Knowing that God has commanded us to be involved in reaching the world with the gospel, we look for ways to help accomplish that task. We know that one thing we can do is give a portion of our financial resources. Based on our expected income we have an idea of how much we can give. Then, based on God's promises, we stretch ourselves out in faith to do even more. We don't know how God will enable us to meet our Faith Promise commitment. But we understand the Promise Principle, and we trust God to enable us as only He can.

Even before Moses and Joshua had experienced God faithfully fulfilling His promises, Abraham was setting the example for them to follow. Paul captures Abraham's example for us in Romans. Abraham was facing an impossible challenge -- becoming a father well passed the age when it was biologically possible. Yet we read, "Against all hope, Abraham believed **just as it had been said to him** ... yet he did not waver through unbelief **regarding the promise of God** ... being fully persuaded that **God had power to do what he had promised** (Romans 4:18,20,21).

This pattern is expanded in the book of Hebrews. Notice carefully the words that describe Abraham's trust. "**By faith Abraham ... was enabled** to become a father because **he considered him faithful who had made the promise** (Hebrews 11:11). That one verse, perhaps more than any other, has all the elements of a Faith Promise. Three key words: faith -- enablement -- promise.

As I put my faith *in God's* promise,
He enables *me to meet the commitment*
He has led me to make.
That, in a sentence, is a Faith Promise.

As I put my **faith** in God's **promise**, He **enables** me to meet the commitment He has led me to make. That, in a sentence, is a Faith Promise.

The Apostle Paul understood this principle well. He boldly declared, "And my God will meet (supply) all your needs according to His glorious riches in Christ Jesus" (Philippians 4:19). This was not just a casual statement by Paul. Nor was it merely a theory he was espousing. He was speaking from the platform of a life that had seen God supply his own needs again and again. As Paul gave himself and his financial resources to meet the needs of others, he discovered that God could meet all of his needs, too. To Paul, it was an experienced fact. His God could and did supply all his need. Paul's personal testimony makes this statement ring with truth.

The unchanging character of God, the same yesterday (Paul's day), today (our day), and forever (Hebrews 13:8), makes Paul's experience relevant to us today. God confirms and authenticates His promise to meet all of our needs by backing it with resources "according to His glorious riches." God's unlimited resources support His claim to meet all our needs.

If I promised to loan you some money "according to my riches," I might be able to muster a few hundred dollars and be able to back it up, according to my riches. If you went to someone like the late Sam Walton, billionaire founder of the Walmart department store chain, to borrow some money "according to his riches," you potentially could borrow millions because his wealth could back it up. But think how much better to come to God, Who owns the cattle on a thousand hills and the very hills themselves, and experience His promised supply "according to His glorious riches."

Jeremiah experienced God's promises firsthand. In chapter 32 of the book that bears his name, Jeremiah prayed to God, rehearsing the high points of Israel's history. In particular he focused on events in Egypt surrounding the people's deliverance, and God's frequent assurances that He would give them the Promised Land. What quickly becomes apparent is the impossible situation in which God's people found themselves. And yet, it happened **exactly** as God said it would **precisely** for that reason – God said it would.

In that same chapter God asks Jeremiah to do an incredible thing. Jerusalem was under attack by the Babylonians. The siege ramps had already been built, the last step in the enemy's battle plan to capture the city. Jeremiah clearly saw the imminent triple danger facing his city: sword, famine, and plague. God had already given Jeremiah a preview of what was going to happen, and none of it was good. "The city will be handed over to the Babylonians who are attacking it ... they will capture it ... and set it on fire ... they will burn it down ... the city will be filled with dead bodies ... the others will be taken captive and banished."

With unspeakable horror on the horizon, and knowing full well what fate awaited his beloved Jerusalem, Jeremiah is told by God to go into the real estate business! He buys a parcel of local (and no doubt bargain-priced) property, knowing the whole area will soon be utterly destroyed by the Babylonians and its people taken captive to Babylon.

To buy a piece of property that you know in advance will fall into enemy hands makes no earthly sense. But obediently Jeremiah buys the property. With the Babylonians hammering away on their siege ramps, and God's words of destruction and captivity ringing in the prophet's ears, Jeremiah completes perhaps the strangest property acquisition in history.

How could Jeremiah do what looked like a totally irresponsible, ridiculous thing? He had a promise. A promise from the Lord. Jeremiah expressed his total trust in what God had said. "Ah, Sovereign Lord, you have made the heavens and the earth by your great power and outstretched arm. Nothing is too hard for you" (Jeremiah 32:17). Jeremiah could confidently trust in His God, because his God had clearly spoken: "This is what the Lord Almighty, the God of Israel, says: Houses, fields and vineyards will again be bought in the land" (32:15).

Jeremiah had the promise of God for the future. Based on this promise, he did not waver in the present, but willingly did what God required by purchasing the land. He knew that the God who could part the Red Sea and plague Egypt's pharaoh, could just as easily do a miracle in a depressed real estate market. Why? Because "nothing is too hard for God."

If Jeremiah had looked only at his present situation, he would not have purchased the land. Nothing external indicated it was a wise thing to do. But in faith -- based upon God's promise – Jeremiah "bought the plot."

Making a Faith Promise is like that. If you look only at your current situation and resources, you will quickly conclude "It's impossible – I can't do it." But if you consider the principle of God's promise, and exercise faith, God will enable you to meet your commitment. Jeremiah did not know exactly how God was going to accomplish everything He had promised to do. But though the prophet didn't know the **how**, he knew the **Who** -- the God who promised that "nothing was too hard for him."

You will never fully trust God's promises until you put yourself in a position where you, like Jeremiah, have to trust them. Making a Faith Promise commitment puts you in that wonderfully vulnerable position. A position you need never fear -- "for He who promised is faithful."

10

Everyone Benefits From Faith Promise

If so many of the churches who have large budgets for missions use the Faith Promise plan, it must have some special positive benefits, not only for the church, but also for the individual members.

When asked about this, pastors and chairpersons of missions committees give several answers.

1. The whole concept of world missions becomes more important and personal.

You always take a more active interest in something if you are financially involved. I once bought a few shares of IBM stock. It was my first venture into the stock market. Before that time, I had no interest in looking at the stock market report in the daily paper. Now I did. And which stock did I look at first? IBM, of course, because I now had a financial interest in its success.

When the missions budget is just one of many line items on a general church budget, it is difficult to generate much personal interest and response to it because there is no definable "point of contact." But with the Faith Promise plan, you have a vital, personal interest and involvement in missions because you have a financial commitment to it. It enables everyone who participates to have a vital role in fulfilling the Great Commission. Missions becomes something as personal and relevant as your checkbook. Seeing the world discipled for Christ becomes a personal priority in the individual's life. The person's whole value system is reordered as he begins to see all that he owns being used for God's purposes.

2. It encourages not only commitment of one's possessions, but also personal commitment of one's life to missionary service.

Many missionaries on the field today developed their first interest in missions by making a Faith Promise commitment. As they started supporting and corresponding with missionaries personally, their own interest in becoming a missionary was aroused. By supporting ministries in other parts of the world, their own desire to help reach that area with the gospel was heightened. They soon found themselves becoming the answer to their own prayers – and it began with a Faith Promise commitment.

3. Everyone can participate.

One of the most exciting dimensions of the Faith Promise is seeing children of all ages make commitments. It might only be 25 cents a month, but it is a start. Think how that level of commitment will grow with the years, having been "planted" in an impressionable young heart at such a tender age.

Older individuals living on small, fixed incomes, can participate, too. Though their involvement may be small in terms of dollars, they can still sense a personal satisfaction in having a part in missions. Young, old, and all ages in between, can participate in the Faith Promise plan for missions giving. Some families may want to consider a "joint" commitment in which the entire family commits to trust God together for a sum of money; other families may find it preferable to encourage each individual member to make his or her own commitment.

4. It encourages planned, systematic giving rather than short-term or emotionally motivated giving.

It is relatively easy to persuade someone to give to a crisis need or life-and-death situation. Famine relief, while certainly a legitimate and worthy need, is an example of something that appeals to our emotions, but in a few days we have often forgotten the reason for our gift. Faith Promise encourages wise planning and giving to missions on a regular basis.

5. Individuals and churches grow spiritually.

When we stretch ourselves in faith, we often find ourselves giving more than we would have simply by habit or expediency. Our spiritual depth and vitality increase. Our faith stretches past its former boundaries into new areas as yet unexplored. Trusting God to meet a Faith Promise commitment encourages us to trust Him in other areas of our daily life.

6. The missions budget becomes a separate part of the church's overall budget.

By having the Faith Promise as a separate category in the church's budget, missions receives more emphasis in the financial life of the church. Otherwise, "Missions" has an uncanny way of getting lost somewhere between "Men's Ministries" and "Music."

7. Faith Promise can revitalize an entire church.

Testimonies from congregation after congregation attest to the fact that financial and spiritual blessing often accompany obedience in the area of giving to missions.

I was in a small church in Pennsylvania for a missions conference. Just a few years before, that church had purchased property and built a new facility. They had borrowed money on a 15-year note to accomplish this energetic task. The year they moved into the new facility, they started the Faith Promise plan of support for missions. Not only did their missions giving increase several fold over all previous years, but they were also able to pay off their 15 year note in only 6 years.

8. Faith Promise provides an opportunity to maintain a year-round interest in missions.

With the possible exception of an annual missions conference or other missions event in your church, the Faith Promise plan is the single most important thing your church can do to keep missions interest high. That way, missions is not limited to an occasional missionary speaker, film or potluck. The Faith Promise emphasis helps maintain interest in missions all year through.

9. Faith Promise develops and deepens the prayer life of the individual members and the church family as a whole.

As individuals are praying daily that God would enable them to meet their Faith Promise, they are also more interested in praying for the unreached peoples of the world, and the missionaries who have dedicated their lives to reach them in this generation.

10. Faith Promise multiplies itself in other churches.

Paul commends the churches in Achaia for their generous gift, telling them "your enthusiasm has stirred most of the other churches to action" (2 Corinthians 9:2). Not only did the people who received the gift directly benefit, but Paul says that their example of giving was used to encourage other churches to give as well. Your experience and blessing from participating in the Faith Promise can be spread to countless other churches so they too will experience the joy of faith giving.

One pastor friend in Pennsylvania, using his church as an example, was able to interest other churches around him to become involved in missions through the Faith Promise. The result: 50 or more churches in his area began having a missions emphasis using the Faith Promise. His interest and enthusiasm stirred others to action as well.

As members move away from a church that is involved in Faith Promise for missions, they too can take the concept, using their enthusiasm to stir the next church. And on and on it goes reproducing itself.

11. Faith Promise helps keep missions in focus during expansion and building programs.

Unfortunately, many times when a church enters into a building program, the missions budget can be decreased considerably with the thought that as soon as the new building is underway and/or paid off, the missions giving can be resumed. A worthy thought, but almost never true. Once missions budgets are decreased they are difficult to get back on track. But churches that faithfully observe the Faith Promise plan of giving to missions, find that they can sustain their giving to missions **along with** their expansion. But perhaps most importantly ...

12. Faith Promise giving pleases God.

Hebrews 11:1 reminds us, "Without faith it is impossible to please God." The Living Bible paraphrases it, "You can never please God without depending on Him." Faith brings joy to the heart of God. As we stretch the boundaries of our faith, not only does our personal spiritual life deepen and expand, but it also pleases our Lord and brings great delight to His heart. The writer of Hebrews amplifies this idea when he says, "And do not forget to do good and to share with others, for with such sacrifice God is pleased" (Hebrews 13:16).

11

Standard Of Living Or Standard Of Giving?

Jack Taylor, in his book *God's Miraculous Plan of Economy*, brings the issue into sharp focus regarding humankind's basic nature. "In the unfallen earth there was plenty of everything, and everything alive in the earth seemed to have one theme. . . GIVE, GIVE, GIVE! The sun gave! The earth gave! The animals gave! Man gave! The trees gave! The glorious giving cycle continued until sin and death reigned. The enemy introduced a new concept into the human spirit...GET, GET, GET! Man became a greedy getter, instead of a gracious giver. He then began to guard...get...keep...hoard."[1]

The September 14, 1987 issue of *Newsweek* magazine carried an article about Bill Cosby, the popular comedian and author. The article centered on the amount of money Cosby was making from his many enterprises – over $50 million a year. *Newsweek* suggested an appropriate headline might be "TV'S FIRST BILLION DOLLAR MAN!" Cosby's first book, for example, was the fastest selling hardcover in publishing history. His second book had a pre-publication order of 1.7 million copies. Add to that his top-rated television program, personal appearances, records and advertising contracts, and you understand *Newsweek's* headline suggestion. What was most revealing was Cosby's answer to a question asked by one reporter: "When does enough become enough?" Cosby's answer reflects the world's system of thought. "No one ever told J. Paul Getty to stop drilling oil wells."

No doubt there are few (if any) reading this book who are in the $50 million a year category. That being true, you may be tempted to think, "I wouldn't be like that! Just give me $1 million and I'll be happy. I wouldn't need or want any more." For a very few, that might be correct. But the reality of the consumptive lifestyle philosophy that pervades our society says otherwise.

It was expressed humorously but accurately at a party where several young couples were discussing the difficulties of family budgets. "I really don't want a lot of money," said one. "I just wish we could afford to live the way we're living now!"

Ron Blue, Managing Partner of the Ronald Blue Company, a Christian financial management group, has been asked many times what is the biggest financial mistake he sees in clients who come for financial help. Without hesitation he responds, "A consumptive lifestyle." Blue defines a consumptive lifestyle as "spending more than you can afford, or spending more than you should, given your other goals and priorities."[2]

God warned against a consumptive lifestyle the very first time He gave the Great Commission. In Genesis 12, God came to Abraham and told him to leave his home, country, and people to go to a new land. If Abraham obeyed, God promised him three things: a blessing of a nation (descendants), a blessing for others who would bless Abraham, and a personal blessing for Abraham himself. But God quickly went on to give the reason for this personal blessing -- **"so that all the families of the earth will be blessed"** (verse 3). Abraham could not consume this blessing upon himself and his people. He had to do something with God's blessing. He had to use it so that all families on earth could be blessed through the Messiah who would come.

The lesson is clear: Abraham could not keep the blessing to himself, or he would lose it. He had to see himself as a channel of that blessing to the whole world.

This same "blessing principle" is seen in many other places in Scripture. Psalm 67 is just one example. Notice the prayer for blessing and then the necessary outflow of that blessing, as you read, "God be merciful to us and **bless us . . . that you may be known on earth, your salvation among all nations."** "God shall bless us, and all the ends of the earth shall fear Him" (verses 1,2,7). The two are inseparable. God blesses, not to make us comfortable, but that we might become a conduit of blessing to others.

The land of Israel has a perfect topographical illustration of this principle. Near the Sea of Galilee everything grows and flourishes. The Sea itself supports a rich variety of marine life. Why? Because it is always giving out. Water constantly flows away from it. Seventy miles due south is another body of water, the Dead Sea. It cannot support any form of life whatsoever. Nothing can grow or prosper there. Why? Because it only takes in but never gives out. Thus the name, Dead Sea.

I am old enough to remember World War II. Many of you are, too. Do you remember the ration stamp books? They are collectors' items now. But back then they were very important. Gas for your car? Frequently in short supply and then only if you had enough stamps. Sugar? Meat? Many times in short supply. Remember margarine? That was my job. To take the plastic bags full of white margarine, and mix the yellow food coloring into them so they would look like "real" butter. But that was all right, because there was a war to fight and win. Everyone was in a war-time frame of mind. You were careful not to waste things. You made do without a new car and other new items. There was a war to win and personal wants and desires were shoved aside.

But then, thankfully, the war ended. The economy started booming. New cars were again available. Television became a necessity of life. And our lifestyle changed, from war-time sacrifice, to peace-time consumption. It didn't happen all at once. But before long it had become an unstoppable force.

Now in our affluence we are bombarded by ads selling us not just a **product**, but a **perspective** on "things." NEW...IMPROVED...AD-VANCED...LATEST...SUPER...are words that scream at us from every aisle and air wave, bombarding our minds, and not so subtly playing on our desire to have **more**, need **more**, want **more**, consume **more**. The attitude being forced upon us can been seen in the headlines of advertisements in our newspapers and magazines:

> "The Secret of Your Success" (an ad for cellular phones).
> "For a Better You -- Luxury You Can Afford" (ad for a beauty salon)
> "You'll Know You've Arrived" (ad for new housing area)
> "62 Ways to Make the Good Life Great" (magazine ad)
> "Go Ahead. You Know You Deserve It" (car ad)
> "Don't You Deserve the Luxury?" (ad for house)
> "See How Easy It Is to Step Up" (car ad)
> "Flights of Fancy and Fantasy Await You" (travel ad)
> "You Can See Your Dreams of a Lifetime Come True with Our Trip" (travel ad)
> "Fine Products -- To Enrich the American Life Style" (merchandise service)

A credit card purchasing service makes this frontal assault on our consumptive lifestyles: "We Know that the Special Items You Would Choose Are Offered Here. And We Make It Easy for You."

Lest we fall victim to the notion that we are immune to such blatant commercialism, consider how often you catch yourself unconsciously humming a tune from some commercial you heard on radio or television. Many times it will be for a product that your Christian convictions wouldn't let you purchase. But you still hum the tune just because you hear it so often. Not too long ago one of the most popular ads had two groups pitted against each other, with one group enthusiastically shouting: "LESS

FILLING!" And the other group shouting back, "T_____ G_____!" You fill in the blanks.

Chuck Swindoll stated it well: "Society's plan of attack is to create dissatisfaction, to convince us that we must be in a constant pursuit for something 'out there' that is sure to bring us happiness. When you reduce that lie to its lowest level, it is saying that contentment is impossible without striving for more."[3]

The consumptive lifestyle is not just something that is spoken about by ministers or missionaries trying to raise money from people who have it but aren't giving. Walt Whitman assailed "the mania of owning things." Thoreau said about material goods, "A man is rich in proportion to the number of things which he can afford to let alone."

In 1993, customers charged $422 billion
on bank credit cards,
a 25% jump from 1992.
In 1993, interest on unpaid balances
rose 16% to $225 billion.
The average family has $2,700 in credit card debt,
versus $1,000 a decade ago.
USA Today, March 12, 1994

An editorial in *U.S. News and World Report* expressed it like this: "In America, to have is to be. To establish that you have succeeded in a society that wants you to acquire as much as possible is to prove the whole experiment was worth the trouble." The editorial went on to say, "To a greater extent than is admitted, one's life is built out of the things one accumulates. Material possessions take on an affective power merely from the fact that they are attached to human beings." The editorial quoted Upton Sinclair, who mused, "Consider Christmas. Could Satan in his most malignant mood have devised a worse combination of graft plus buncombe than the system whereby several hundred million people get a billion or so gifts for which they have no use and some thousands of shop clerks die of exhaustion while selling them...all in the name of Jesus?"[4]

Most of us, if we were honest, would have to admit we live a consumptive lifestyle, and we have the credit debt to prove it. According to the Internal Revenue Service, the average American pays $8,000 a year in interest to lending institutions. That same "average American" also has over $2,000 floating around in credit card debts.

Credit cards have become a way of life and in the process have also made debt the "American way of life." Why save for that stereo or vacation when, by merely signing at the X, you can have it now. This idea was expressed in bold letters in a full page ad in *USA Today* telling about a new, Platinum credit card. The headline read: "Sometimes the greatest reward of personal recognition is **instant gratification**." The result of having it now? The average American's installment debt has grown from $239 in 1960 to $2,700 in 1993.

At the same time consumer debt was increasing 1100%, average giving to the church dropped to 2.79% of income. Would it be safe to assume there is a connection between the **increase** in consumer debt, and the **decrease** in giving to the church? The conclusion is inescapable.

> *At the same time consumer debt*
> *was increasing 1100%*
> *average giving to the church dropped*
> *to 2.79% of income.*
> *Would it be safe to assume there is a connection*
> *between the increase in consumer debt,*
> *and the decrease in giving to the church?*
> *The conclusion is inescapable.*

An article in the *Readers Digest* entitled "Plastic Is as Good as Gold," added this: "For many Americans, charging a purchase has become too easy. The old restraint on buying -- lack of cash -- no longer exists, and millions of people are over their head in credit debt. Research proves what we know from experience: credit-card possession increases impulse spending.

"Boston bankruptcy attorney Joseph Mooney says that the easy availability of credit cards is one of the main reasons personal bankruptcies there have risen 35% since 1985."[5]

The more I read and hear, the more convinced I become that this is true. A financial planner was hosting a phone-in radio talk show I was listening to recently while driving back from Alabama. Some people were calling for investment advice, but the most common call was from people wanting to know how to get out of debt. I was shocked to hear one lady saying she and her husband had accumulated $15,000 in debt, mostly on credit cards.

A newspaper article I read talked about a lady who had $12,000 in credit card debt. She admitted, "I liked to go to specialty shops where they would call me by my name as I walked through the door." Then she added, "It gave me a feeling of self worth." (And, I might add, it gave the store a nice net worth.) The article went on to say that the lady "jokes that at least her trip to bankruptcy court was made in style, thanks to the dresses and more than 200 pairs of shoes she charged."

The National Foundation for Consumer Credit says about 2 percent of the 130 million Americans who buy on credit are "mired" in credit-card debt, 4 percent face "some difficulties," and 10 percent experience "some discomfort." A financial counselor paints an even gloomier picture. "The average person counseled at our office (Shopper Stoppers Foundation) in 1980 had around $9,500 in accumulated debt. In 1988 the figure had almost doubled, to $17,000." She added, "Credit-card debt is the fastest growing component of overall consumer debt."[6]

John Wesley's lifestyle practices and priorities were radical, even by 18th century standards. His views would make us uncomfortable, were he living and preaching today.

As Wesley ministered, he would strive to limit his expenses so that he had more money to give to charity. He records that one year his income was 30 pounds and his living expenses 28 pounds, so he had 2 pounds to give away. The next year his income doubled but he still managed to live on 28 pounds, so he had 32 pounds to give to charity. In the third year, his income jumped to 90 pounds. Instead of letting his expenses rise with his income, he kept them to 28 pounds, and gave away 62 pounds. In the fourth year he received 120 pounds. As before, his expenses were kept to 28 pounds so his giving rose to 92 pounds.

Wesley continued this austere lifestyle throughout his 87 years. One year his income was over 1,400 pounds. He lived on 30 pounds that year and gave away the rest -- a "tithe" of nearly 98%!

How was this possible? Wesley's philosophy was simple. He limited his expenditures by not purchasing many of the items thought essential for a man of his station in life. As an Oxford graduate, a brilliant intellectual, a Greek scholar, and the man credited with helping to bring the Great Awakening to America and the Industrial Revolution to England, Wesley was highly respected. Nonetheless, he urged Christians to buy only the necessities of life. "When people spend money on things they do not really need, they begin to want more things they do not need." Wesley believed that "with increasing income, what should rise is not the Christian's standard of living, but the standard of giving."[7]

Now, you might be saying, "Yes, but Wesley lived in another world, 200 years removed from mine. He didn't know anything about double-digit inflation, high interest rates, and commuting an hour each way to work." We conclude, therefore, that Wesley's thinking and lifestyle wouldn't work today.

True, it is another day and age. But does that necessarily mean Wesley's ideals are out of date? Or is it that we just aren't interested in his kind of commitment?

Regardless of the century, Wesley's basic approach **will** work today if we are serious about not living a consumptive lifestyle, in order to better reach the world with the gospel. Robertson McQuilkin put things squarely in perspective when he said, "We live in an age when we are easily blinded by preoccupation with self-fulfillment so that we cannot see the world as God sees it."[8]

> *"When people spend money on things*
> *they do not really need,*
> *they begin to want more things*
> *they do not need.*
> *With increasing income,*
> *what should rise is not the Christian's*
> *standard of living,*
> *but the standard of giving."*
> **John Wesley**

The great tragedy for most is that this consumptive lifestyle puts them in bondage to debt. There is a sobering reality that we must face. "Debt and lifestyle go hand in hand in American society. When you use debt to fund a consumptive lifestyle, not only do you have the consumptive lifestyle working against you financially, but you also have the additional burden of the debt working against you financially. Both should be avoided like the plague."[9]

Financial management experts (both secular and Christian) tell us to avoid a consumptive lifestyle and its accompanying debt burden. Does Scripture support their advice? The answer is apparent to any who will but make a cursory inspection of Scripture.

Psalm 112:5,9 teaches us that the righteous man is one who is "generous, and who scatters his gifts to the poor, and in so doing his righteousness will endure forever."

Proverbs 11:24,25 reminds us that "One man gives freely, yet gains even more; another withholds unduly, but comes to poverty. A generous man will prosper; he who refreshes others will himself be refreshed."

Matthew 6:21, "Where your treasure is, there your heart will be also." The use of our resources is directly tied to our heart's priorities. Or to put it another way, show me your checkbook and I'll tell you what is really important in your life.

Ecclesiastes 5:13,14 supports this notion: "I have seen a grievous evil under the sun: wealth hoarded to the harm of its owner, or wealth lost through some misfortune."

Luke 14:33, "In the same way, any of you who does not give up everything he has cannot be my disciple." Chuck Swindoll amplifies the meaning of that verse. "In today's vernacular, committed individuals live with shallow tent pegs. They may own things, but nothing owns them. They have come to terms with merchandise that has a price tag and opted for commitments to value that are priceless."[10]

Luke 12:48 provides this sobering warning: "From everyone who has been given much, much will be demanded; and from the one who has been entrusted with much, much more will be asked." I know, as Americans, we get tired of hearing about all of our affluence as compared to much of the world. But the stubborn facts won't go away. We are rich by any standard you care to employ. These words from Luke should sting deeply and remind us of God's perspective on our abundance.

We are all familiar with the story in Luke 16:19-31 of the rich man and Lazarus. William Barclay reminds us of the main lesson in the story. "It is a terrible warning to remember that the sin of the rich man was, **not that he did wrong things, but that he did nothing.**"[11]

1 Timothy 6:17-19 admonishes us, "Command those who are rich...to do good, to be rich in good deeds, and to be generous and willing to share. In this way they will lay up treasure for themselves...so that they may take hold of the life that is truly life."

There is a line in the Jewish Talmud that reads: "Man is born with his hands clenched; he dies with them wide open. Entering life, he desires to grasp everything; leaving the world, all he possessed has slipped away."[12]

There is only one way to combat all of this consumptive lifestyle that is pressed upon us from all sides. We must make personal choices regarding our lifestyle, our values, and our priorities that cut contrary to the world's system and free us to use our resources to help reach the world with the gospel. It takes a disciplined will to voluntarily place limits on ourselves to reduce and control our spending. Is that easy? No, of course not. But it is something that pleases God and extends His kingdom on earth.

Legend has it that a man was lost in the desert, dying for a drink of water. He stumbled upon an old shack -- a ramshackle, windowless, roofless, weather-beaten old shack. He looked about the place and found a little shade from the heat of the desert sun. As he glanced around he saw a pump about fifteen feet away -- an old rusty water pump. He stumbled over to it, grabbed the handle, and began to pump up and down, up and down. Nothing happened.

Disappointed, he staggered back. He noticed off to the side an old jug. He looked at it, wiped away the dirt and dust, and read a message that said, "You have to prime the pump with all the water in this jug, my friend. P.S. Be sure you fill the jug again before you leave."

He popped the cork out of the jug and sure enough, there was water. Almost a jug full. Suddenly, he was faced with a decision. If he drank the water, he might live a bit longer. Ah, but if he followed the instructions and poured all the water down the old rusty pump, it just might yield fresh, cool water from deep down in the well -- all the water he wanted and needed.

He studied the possibilities, and weighed the options. What should he do? Pour out the little he had and take a chance? Or drink what was in the old jug and ignore its message. Should he risk it all...or consume it all?

Reluctantly, he poured all the water into the pump. Then he grabbed the handle and began to pump...squeak, squeak, squeak. Still nothing came out! Squeak, squeak, squeak. A little bit began to dribble out, then a small stream, and finally a gushing fountain. To his relief, fresh, cool water poured out of the rusty pump. Eagerly, he filled the jug and drank from it. He filled it another time and once again drank its refreshing contents.

Then he filled the jug for the next traveler. He filled it to the top, popped the cork back on, and added this little note: "Believe me, it really works. YOU HAVE TO GIVE IT ALL AWAY BEFORE YOU CAN GET ANYTHING BACK."[13]

In light of the Great Commission and the needs of the world all around us, we have a choice to make. Jim Elliott made his choice and expressed it this way: "He is no fool, who gives what he cannot keep, to gain what he cannot lose."

May God grant us the grace to **live below** our means, that we might **give above** what we would otherwise be able to for His kingdom purposes.

12

Misconceptions About Faith Promise

With every good plan or program, misconceptions and misunder-standings are sure to arise. The same is true with the Faith Promise plan. Keep the following thoughts in mind, therefore, as you consider making a Faith Promise commitment.

1. "I can't consider making a Faith Promise until I'm in a better financial position. Perhaps in the future, but not now."

Individuals will often say "I plan to make a Faith Promise just as soon as...my children get through college...we get our car paid off...I get a better job...I receive my inheritance from my parents...I recover from my 'unfortunate' investment...I get my retirement plan vested."

Pastors use a similar line of argument: "I know the value of a Faith Promise commitment to missions. And believe me, we will be making one as a church someday. We have some long range plans, and missions is definitely a part of them. We have aggressive plans to pay off our mort-gage -- we want to re-pave our parking lots -- we need to upgrade the church's computer -- the choir needs new robes -- we have plans to buy another church van. But we have some good financial counselors on our church board and they tell me we can do everything we have planned, and pay for it in just six more years. **Then** we can really start giving to missions."

I have news for you. It will never happen. "One of these days" is "none of these days." This concept of "just as soon as" giving reminds me of a poem I memorized once:

> The bride bent with age, leaned over her cane,
> Her steps uncertain need guiding.
> While down the church aisle, with a wan toothless smile,
> The groom in a wheel chair gliding.

>   And who is this elderly couple thus wed?
>   You'll find when you've closely explored it,
>   That this is that rare, most conservative pair,
>   **Who waited 'till they could afford it.**[1]

Perhaps the late Peter Marshall expressed it best when he said, "We had better give according to our income, lest God make our income according to our giving." Our giving is to be proportionate to what we have -- not what we hope to have when we are in a better financial position sometime in the future.

Consider the widow in Mark 12, who, in spite of being in extreme poverty herself, gave all she had. Frank Barker uses her story to challenge us to take "faith risks." "Are you in poverty? Perhaps, like this widow, your situation is hilariously impossible. She couldn't live on a mere penny, just as you can't possibly make it on the resources you have. Some will encourage you to plead, 'I'm so poor I have nothing to give.' But don't listen to them! Don't wait until you think you have 'enough' to be able to give. Giving isn't an issue of convenience; it's a matter of faith. **Whatever keeps you from giving when you're poor, will also keep you from giving when you're rich.**"[2]

2. Faith Promise is not a cure-all for a church budget that is already in the red.

The temptation upon hearing of other churches who use the Faith Promise plan and whose local budget has doubled or tripled, is to conclude, "What have we got to lose? We'll start the Faith Promise, and our local budget will automatically grow." Generally, there is growth in the local budget in churches that use the Faith Promise plan. But other factors are equally important for a strong budget.

The motive for using the Faith Promise must be as an aid to help your congregation focus on world missions, **not** merely to increase the local budget. The focus is outward. If, in the process, God chooses to bless you locally as well, wonderful! But a Faith Promise is not a magic cure-all for your local budget problems.

3. Faith Promise is not a cure-all for personal problems -- financial, physical, family, or spiritual.

The logic runs something like this: "If I make a Faith Promise, then all my personal problems will be solved. Surely, if I become involved in missions, God won't let me down in other areas." Or a person will hear a testimony of someone who made a Faith Promise for $1,000 and during the year his business doubled and he received a $2,000 bonus, which covered his Faith Promise and gave him $1,000 extra. Upon hearing such a testimony, many are tempted to think, "I'll try it! I'll make a Faith

Promise, and God will double my business this year. I'll get a big bonus so I'll have more money for myself."

Jesus told His disciples on one occasion to get into the boat, go to the other side of the lake, and wait for Him there. They climbed into the boat, set sail, and what happened? The boat almost sank, and they nearly drowned. Doing what? **Doing exactly what Jesus had told them to do.** In the same way, simple obedience to God's leading in making a Faith Promise commitment does not guarantee success and health.

Permit me a personal word. The year my wife and I gave more to missions than ever before, we had the highest medical bills in our entire married lives. Or consider the experience of some dear friends who for years had made very generous Faith Promises, and had also been very active on the missions committee of their church. The year the husband was selected to be chairman of the missions committee, his business collapsed, and the family lost everything except their house (which they were able to keep because of generous friends who shared with them.) The husband was out of a job; his wife went back to work to keep food on the table. They are just now -- three years later -- starting to recover from the experience. Making a large Faith Promise in no way guarantees a cure-all for personal problems.

4. National and international economic realities don't go away.

Simply because thousands of people in America make Faith Promises does not guarantee national economic stability. We still live in a sin-cursed world. Tragedies do occur. Stock markets do crash. Employee layoffs do happen. Businesses do close. Farmers do lose their land. Incomes do suddenly disappear. People do retire. Things happen over which we have no control. Many times these impact our ability to give. But God is still God. Our faith is still faith. And God honors commitment even in difficult economic times.

5. Faith Promise is not a cure-all for financial mismanagement, poor business decisions, or lax work habits.

If I make a Faith Promise, God is under no obligation to rearrange bad investments to suddenly make me wealthy. Nor is God under any obligation to set aside my sloppy lifestyle or lax work habits, and in spite of myself, to provide the money. A Faith Promise is no substitute for honest hard work and careful business practices.

6. Faith Promise is not a substitute for the tithes and offerings God expects me to give to my local church.

Some churchgoers who do not tithe, for example, occasionally drop a dollar or two in the plate to salve their consciences. Then a Faith Promise opportunity comes along. Here is the solution to their guilty feelings over not giving. They make a Faith Promise, which is perhaps the amount their tithe should have been. They don't see any supply for their Faith Promise during the year. Then they rationalize, "Well, I tried. It's not my fault I couldn't give more this year, because God didn't give me any money for my Faith Promise. I certainly would have given it if God had supplied it. But He never did." And in the whole process, not only did they not give anything for a Faith Promise, they did not even tithe. But their conscience feels better because at least "I tried...God just didn't come through for me."

7. Faith Promise is not an excuse to start a business so I can give the profits to God.

Consider the case of the person who says, "If God will prosper my business, then I'll give." History shows that those whose businesses have prospered were already giving and continued to give regularly in the "lean" times as well as the good. Some first-time participants in the Faith Promise reason that they will go into business, and "help the Lord out" if the business prospers by giving the profits to meet their Faith Promise commitment. Sadly, only a few have done this and been faithful to give back to the Lord regularly, both in the lean times as well as the good. The danger is that most stop giving altogether, waiting for God "to send prosperity, so we can give a lot." It's a subtle but real temptation to keep investing all the profits back into the business to build up an even larger amount to give.

Many investors believe it makes good sense to keep the investment dollars and their earnings, in order to make additional investments and (someday) give more to the Lord's work. Ron Blue disagrees. "This rationale is unscriptural because God expects a portion of the increase. Proverbs 3:9-10 leaves no room for argument." ("Honor the Lord with your wealth, with the first fruits of all your crops; **then** your barns will be filled to overflowing and your vats will brim over with new wine.") Blue adds, "To put off giving under the assumption that the investment will earn more and then you will have more to give is a great danger. This assumption implies that God is incapable of using His money today, for a greater eternal impact than what I can do by investing."[3]

People who start businesses with the idea of making money to support God's causes, but who do not give regularly through the bad times as well as the good, rarely ever succeed. Give regularly and what is expected, whether God prospers you or not.

13

Beyond The Faith Promise

I was in a friend's office one day who owns a very successful business. In a cabinet he keeps a supply of various items as sales promotions. He went to the cabinet, opened it, and said, "Here, could you use this?" and handed me a beautiful Seiko wall clock. He pulled out two very nice nylon jackets and said, "Why don't you take these, too. Give one to your wife." From another shelf he handed me two boxes of golf balls. I finally said, "I'm embarrassed for you to give me all of this." He smiled very kindly, and then graciously said, "Don't rob me of the joy of giving."

His giving far exceeds golf balls and wall clocks. His church, many mission causes, and other worthy charities have all been the recipients of his spiritual gift of giving.

A missionary was trying to pick up the tab for a meal with a Christian businessman friend who is very generous with his giving and hospitality. The missionary said, "Lou, you do so much for us missionaries, let me do this for you." His businessman friend who doesn't mince words, replied, "I don't tell you how to run your ministry, so don't try to tell me how to run mine." Missionaries and mission causes all over the world have benefited from this businessman's generosity -- a generosity that far exceeds picking up tabs for meals.

Earlier we looked at the consumptive lifestyle attitude that presses itself on us from all sides. We defined a consumptive lifestyle by borrowing Ron Blue's words: it is "spending more than you can afford, or spending more than you should, given your other goals and priorities."

But we need to be honest. Many people in our churches today **can** afford it. They can afford a new car every year. They can afford a new house. They can afford to take trips around the world to exotic places, and frequently do. These are people who have substantial means, obtained by a combination of inheritance, hard work, success in business, and wise investments. Many of these people **do** give significant sums to missions already. How then does a Faith Promise commitment relate to them?

We frequently use illustrations of the different ways God enables people to meet their Faith Promise. We all thrill at the testimony of the person living on a modest retirement, who receives an unexpected insurance refund of $300, which is the exact amount of his Faith Promise commitment. But some in the church cannot relate to that story at all. They have the means to write a check for $300 -- or $3,000 -- or $30,000 for that matter, and not even have to check their bank balance first. For them, giving has another dimension.

> *"The whole teaching of the Christian ethic is,*
> *not that wealth is a sin,*
> *but that wealth is a very great responsibility."*
> **William Barclay**

This chapter is written primarily for those who fall into one of two categories:

1. Christians who have substantial amounts of money, and who give as God has prospered them.

Not every church has people like that, of course. But increasingly here in the United States, a growing number of Christians are becoming financially successful and independently wealthy. Some of these people have inherited wealth. Others have worked long, hard hours, demonstrating faithfulness and diligence in their financial management. Many have made wise investments through the years and accumulated property and portfolios of substantial net worth. A few just seem to have that "midas" touch. For whatever reason, many Christians today have considerable financial assets, and they are using their wealth to advance the kingdom of God.

2. Christians in high income brackets, making far more than the average, who do not give much to the cause of Christ.

These people have the potential to give substantial amounts for advancing the cause of world evangelization, if only they would catch the vision and **do some wise financial planning**.

In Paul's list of spiritual gifts, he tucks the gift of giving right in there with prophecy, faith, and leadership. (By the way, have you ever noticed that when people talk about praying for or desiring certain spiritual gifts, there is a strange silence when it comes to desiring or praying for the gift of giving?)

Paul tells Timothy to "command those who are rich in this present world..." and then lists things they should and should not do because of their wealth. They should not be "arrogant or trust in their wealth." But they should "put their hope in God, do good, be rich in good deeds, and be generous and willing to share" (1 Timothy 6:17,18).

Remember now, Paul's charge was given to "those who are rich in this present world." We might think of the early church as made up completely of poor people and slaves. True, there were many. But here we see that even in the early church, some had substantial financial resources, enough for Paul to describe them as "rich." It's interesting to note that they are not condemned at all for having money. Paul is telling them what to do and not to do with their money. But nowhere does he condemn them for having money in the first place. Paul tells them not to become proud of the fact they have money, not to put their hope in their money. But neither are they to abandon their money. Instead, they are to use their money to do good things in a generous, willing spirit.

William Barclay provides this comment about Paul's instruction: "The whole teaching of the Christian ethic is, not that wealth is a sin, but that wealth is a very great responsibility. If a man's wealth ministers to nothing but his own pride and enriches no one but himself, then his wealth becomes his ruination, because it has impoverished his soul. Every time we could have given and did not give, lessens the wealth that is laid up for us in the world to come; every time we gave of what we had increases the riches that are laid up for us when this life comes to an end."[1]

Neither does Jesus condemn people for having money. In the so-called Parable of the Talents, the only person who is condemned as being wicked and lazy (i.e., unproductive with what God had given him) is the person who did not show a profit. Jesus commended the other two because they had invested wisely the money they had been given. Jesus was pleased with those who had worked hard and increased their wealth. Of the one whom He condemned, He said, "At least you could have put your money on deposit with the bankers, so that when I returned I would have received it back with interest" (Matthew 25:27). Jesus was saying, "The bank doesn't pay a lot, but at least it pays something. You were wrong for not investing in others what I entrusted to you."

In short, **what you keep, you lose; what you give, you gain.**

God has chosen to bless some people with vast wealth, and others with incomes much higher than the average person. Chuck Swindoll put it in perspective when he wrote, "You are neither suspect nor guilty in God's eyes simply because you are rich. You are greatly blessed, and that carries with it great responsibility. As the object of innumerable attacks from the adversary (not to mention the envy of many people) you must be a wise servant of what God has entrusted into your care."

God never condemns those who have money ethically obtained. God's concern is what they **do** with what they **have**. He desires them to "do good, to be rich in good deeds, and to be generous and willing to share."

The Apostle Paul expressed this principle another way: "Now it is required that those who have been given a trust, must prove faithful" (1 Corinthians 4:2). Many Christians in our churches today have been given a trust of money. God desires that they prove faithful with that special trust.

One of the best examples of a person using his money for the Lord is Stanley Tam. After being in business for ten years, Tam felt God asking for 51% of the growing company to be turned over to Him. You can imagine the surprise when Tam went to an attorney asking him to draw up legal papers turning over 51% of his business to God. The attorney refused. Eventually, another attorney agreed to help with this strange request to set up Tam's company with God as "majority stockholder."

Five years later the contract was changed giving God 60% ownership. A few years after that Mr. Tam was speaking in Colombia, South America on a mission trip. During the invitation he was extending to others to receive Christ as Savior, Tam sensed God was speaking to his own heart about a further step of obedience and commitment. The commitment? To give God 100% ownership of the stock in his company, making Tam an employee of his own company.

For several years now a foundation has controlled the company's assets. Tam is paid a salary like any regular employee. God owns 100% of the stock, and all the profits go to the Lord's work, with the major portion designated for overseas missionary outreach.

Did his business become a booming overnight success after he made that initial commitment of 51%? By no means. By his own admission Tam "faced many tests, some of them excruciating." Not only did he have many business ups and downs, sleepless nights, and heartbreaking setbacks, but at one point Tam seriously considered looking for other employment to supplement his income. In addition to business and financial tests, God put him through numerous spiritual battles involving restitution and legal disputes.

Through it all Tam has maintained his commitment, and God has honored him and his business, allowing him to give substantial amounts of money to support Christian ministries around the world.[2]

R. G. LeTourneau, designer and manufacturer of heavy earth-moving equipment, is a name familiar to most American Christians today. I once had the privilege of hearing him share his testimony about being in business partnership with God. He told how his machinery transformed 5,000 acres of marsh land into New York's Idlewild (now Kennedy) Airport, tore open the wilderness for the Alaskan highway, made airstrips for the landing of the first Allied fighter planes on the beaches of Normandy on D-Day, and cleared the debris from bombed-out European cities after World War II.

In the early years of his business, LeTourneau went into partnership with God. "Because I believe that God wants businessmen as well as preachers to be His servants," he said, "I believe that a factory can be dedicated to His service as well as a church." In 1935 Le Tourneau irrevocably assigned over 90% of the company's profits to the LeTourneau Foundation, described as a "Not-for-Profit Corporation whose income and capital can be used only for the cause of Christ."

> *God never condemns those*
> *who have money ethically obtained.*
> *God's concern is what they do with what they have.*
> *He desires them to "do good,*
> *to be rich in good deeds,*
> *and to be generous and willing to share."*

Countless Christian schools and organizations have been the recipients of his gift of giving. Scarcely a mission field exists on all five continents where some devoted worker has not been aided through money from this foundation. Altogether, millions of dollars have been given to further the Lord's work.[3]

These two examples, and many other men and women just like them, have done what Paul exhorted those who had been given a similar trust: they have "proved faithful." They have been astute in their business practices and have carefully and wisely structured their financial affairs in order to give the maximum amount to the church and other related Christian ministries.

Tam and LeTourneau are examples of wealthy Christians who give substantial sums to promote the cause of Christ. But for every example like that, there are hundreds of Christians in the second category with above-average incomes who have the **potential** to give, but are not presently giving. Why might that be? There are usually one or two reasons for this:

1. Christians do not have the high level of commitment required to give.

There is an interesting change that occurs in our giving patterns as we start "moving up" the income ladder. I talked to a successful doctor one day who expressed it very well. "It's interesting," he said. "When we were in med-school, just barely squeaking by from one pay check to the next, we somehow found it easier to tithe than we do now. Back then, our tithe was maybe $600 or $700 a year. But as I started my practice, all of a sudden our tithe wasn't $600 a year anymore, but $1,000, then $2,000, and then it kept creeping on up in the $3,000 and $4,000 and $5,000 range. Suddenly, that seemed like a lot of money -- and it was. And for some reason, even though I was making a lot more than when I was in med-school, it became increasingly more difficult to give even a tithe, much less additional offerings."

That's what I mean about needing a high level of commitment to give. Many in our churches today **do** have good paying jobs and are making handsome salaries. When you get to the point where a **tithe** of your income is as much as the entire **salary** many people make, it takes a high level of commitment to give those amounts to the Lord.

It boils down to priorities, doesn't it? The sad truth is that giving is a low priority for most Christians. Americans are probably the most generous people in the world, giving billions of dollars each year to charities. But are we really **that** generous? Is giving an important priority for us?

According to a Gallup poll it is a rare American family that gives 10% to anything. Only 9 percent of U.S. households gave 5% or more. One-third gave less than 1%. Nearly 29% gave nothing. Interestingly, the poll said, "You might guess that the low givers are mostly lower-income people who are finding it tough just to pay their bills. Not so! In general, the higher one's income, the lower the percentage given to charity." The article goes on to say, "If you have been giving 1 or 2 percent of your income, 5 or 10 percent may sound like an impossible stretch. But some families in every income group manage to donate 5% or more to help others or to support a cause. **It's a question of priorities.**"[4]

But those figures are for all households -- Christian and non-Christian. Certainly we Christians do much better than the national average, don't we? In a survey reported in *Moody Magazine,* the facts and trends are not that encouraging. From 1968 to 1985, Americans' disposable income **increased 31%**. At the same time the percentage of income given per member to their church **decreased 8.5%**. The study determined that the average church member gave 3.05% of disposable income to the church in 1968, but only 2.79% in 1985. Researcher Sylvia Ronsvalle said, "What we found essentially is that people are placing a higher value on their life styles than on their church. **People have more disposable income to spend, but they are finding places other than church to spend it.**"[5]

Those in this second group do give -- some. But they don't usually come close to giving in proportion to the way God has blessed them.

That is the basis of the principle of giving set forth in Acts 11:29, where it says that they gave "each according to his ability." That is the yardstick God uses when He looks at our checking accounts and investment portfolios.

From his experience in financial planning, Ron Blue suggests three basic reasons why Christians fail to give properly.

• **Christians don't give because they don't know how.**

Many people don't realize there are a variety of ways to give without disrupting cash flow, such as giving away appreciated property, or establishing trusts, private foundations, and community foundations. Most of these avenues of giving may require expert advice.

• **Christians don't give because they don't know how much they have.**

They have no idea how much they have, so they don't realize how much they can give.

• **Christians don't give because they don't plan to give.**

"Most of us are responders in our giving habits. Rather than determining a long-range giving plan, we wait until urgent needs are presented to us and then react to them. After working with our clients on a fairly intensive basis to develop a plan that reflects their desire to give, some have been able to increase their giving four times without an increase in income."[6]

That points up yet another reason why those who have the potential for giving substantial amounts, don't.

2. Christians do not use sound financial planning.

I certainly would not presume in the space of a few pages to outline a financial management plan. In the first place, it would take much more space than is possible in the scope of this book. In the second place, I am in no way qualified to speak on the subject of financial management. Many fine Christian financial planners can assist you. An assortment of excellent books, cassettes, and videotapes are available on the subject.

To point up the importance of sound financial planning, Ron Blue shared the following story about one of his first clients. "He was a physician, age 50, who made $85,000 a year and had a net worth of $350,000. When asked about his long-term goals, he replied that he wanted to be financially independent within five years so he could use his skills on the mission field. Another goal was to give $1 million (to charity) before the end of his life.

"When we looked at his income and net worth, those goals seemed unrealistic. But weeks later, after his financial plan was completed, he was asked, 'How would you like to retire in five years, and be financially independent?' He answered, 'That would be terrific!' 'Very well, how would you also like to give away a million dollars during the same five year period?' He was flabbergasted! How did it happen? It was no miracle; practical steps were taken and as a result, in the past few years he met both his goals. Because the doctor's net worth was actually quite a bit more than he thought, it was relatively simple to meet his goals."[7]

The whole point is that the doctor did have the potential to give much more than the average, but he wasn't doing so because of inadequate financial planning.

To repeat, giving "beyond a Faith Promise" has two requirements:

(1) A level of commitment that treats giving as a first priority, and
(2) Sound, professional financial planning.

If you don't plan to give, you won't give. Being a wise steward in the management of your God-given resources requires preparation and planning. Rarely will it happen automatically.

Perhaps in the final analysis, all this isn't really "beyond Faith Promise" after all. If I sit down today and have a desire to give substantial sums to the Lord's work over the next year, or five years, or even my entire lifetime, that does require a lot of faith, doesn't it?

Faith in the future. Faith in my financial advisors. Faith in the economy. Faith in my ability to earn money. And most of all – faith in God, the One Who alone can enable me to reach my full potential as a steward of His resources.

Appendix A
How To Make A Faith Promise

How do you go about making a Faith Promise? Is there a formula you should follow? Is there a process to observe? Are there clearly defined steps you should take?

As you read about Faith Promise or listen to a presentation by a missions speaker, you discover there is probably no "best" way to make a Faith Promise. But there are certain principles which need to be recognized and observed in order for the Faith Promise to be meaningful and understood.

Abraham's example of faith recorded in Genesis 12, Romans 4, and Hebrews 11 can serve as a good "How To" as we consider making a Faith Promise commitment.

1. Pray for God's direction.

Abraham was a man of prayer, who "called upon the name of the Lord" everywhere he sojourned. Genesis 12:1 begins, "The Lord had said to Abram...." We can assume that God and Abraham had been in conversation. We're not told exactly how this occurred. But we can assume that Abraham had been praying to God and God had spoken to him, giving instructions regarding what he should do.

The same principle applies to making a Faith Promise. Much prayer should precede it. There is much more to making a Faith Promise that having your memory jogged on the Sunday that the Faith Promise cards are collected. Grabbing a card, jotting down the first number that pops into your head, and tossing the card into the offering plate is a far cry from fellowshipping with God in prayer and communion, seeking His mind regarding what commitment He would have you to make.

Making a Faith Promise is a spiritual exercise. It should be preceded – and completed -- by prayer. Prayer to discern the amount of your commitment, and prayer for God's enabling help in fulfilling your commitment.

2. Make a realistic assessment of your situation.

"Against all hope...(Abraham) faced the fact..." (Romans 4:18,19). The passage goes on to remind us what those important and impossible facts were: "...his body was as good as dead – since he was about 100 years old -- and that Sarah's womb was also dead." Today we marvel at women giving birth in their late 40's or early 50's. Abraham faced not one impossibility but two: he was too old to father a child, and he was married to a woman who was too old to mother one.

The point is, Abraham honestly faced the facts of life.

When it comes to making a Faith Promise we should keep this in mind. Faith is not some blind, unrealistic, presumptuous leap into space. There are facts that we need to face. For example, if you have just graduated from college, are beginning your first job, and still owe thousands of dollars in school loans, those are facts you need to face. It would not be realistic for you to make a Faith Promise of $10,000.

Now, before you pick up your pen to write and tell me that I am being inconsistent when I use the words "Faith Promise" and "realistic" in the same sentence, let me hasten to add a word of explanation. A student in Washington who owed a substantial amount for school loans, nonetheless made a sizeable Faith Promise. Later that year a family member died, leaving the student with enough money to pay off all the student loans, and fulfill the entire Faith Promise commitment. Yes, that kind of "miracle" does occur. But it should be noted carefully that people who do have an unusual supply like that, usually only have it once in a lifetime.

Perhaps a guideline would be helpful here. As you pray about your Faith Promise over a period of time, and honestly face the facts of your particular situation, if you still have a deep conviction that God is impressing on you to make a Faith Promise commitment that seems totally unrealistic, then you should probably make the commitment and trust God. But be sure that you, like Abraham, have first "faced the facts."

3. Obey God's voice.

"By faith Abraham, when called to go to a place...obeyed and went" (Hebrews 11:8). God was asking Abraham to do an incredible thing. With nothing to cling to but his faith in God, Abraham launched out"...even though he did not know where he was going" (Hebrews 11:18).

Making a Faith Promise requires similar obedience. Many times after we have prayed about our Faith Promise amount, the figure that God impresses upon us seems totally impossible. At that point, we must check to make sure we know what God is saying, and then, in total obedience to Him, make our commitment.

It is the testimony of many that "my hand trembled as I filled out the Faith Promise card and wrote in the amount. I knew there was absolutely no way I could meet that commitment unless God helped me."

Jill Briscoe is right: "Take some risks. If you're not pressured to trust God, you won't."[1]

4. Trust God.

"Against all hope, Abraham in hope believed...without weakening in his faith...yet he did not waver through unbelief...but was strengthened in his faith" (Romans 4:18,19,20).

Abraham completely trusted God, even though humanly speaking his situation was hopeless. William Barclay reminds us, "The essence of Abraham's faith in this case was that he believed that God could make the impossible possible."[2] "Abraham obeyed the summons to go out to a place which he would eventually possess" (Hebrews 11:8, Phillips). If Abraham had already lived in the land it would have required no faith. But he was not there yet. In fact, he didn't even know where the land was. But Abraham trusted God so completely, he knew that if God had **promised** it, it was only a matter of time before he **possessed** it.

It was not the **size** of Abraham's faith that determined the outcome, but rather the **object** of his faith. His God had promised it would happen; his God had the power to make it happen. Therefore, Abraham could relax in the arms of his all-knowing, all-powerful God.

5. Look for God's enablement to meet your Faith Promise commitment.

Abraham was "enabled" to become a father because God performed a miracle. Generally, there are three ways God "enables" us to meet our Faith Promise commitments. (Refer to Chapters 3,4,5.)

6. Be faithful to give as God enables you.

Several times in Scripture we read of Abraham's faithfulness to do what God instructed him. "So Abraham left...so Abraham built an altar...so Abraham went up from Egypt...so Abraham moved his tent...Abraham got up and saddled his donkey...Abraham reached out his hand to take his knife" (Genesis 12:4; 13:1,18; 22:2,3).

Not only did Abraham believe God could do what He had promised, Abraham continually demonstrated his trust by faithfully carrying out God's instructions to him.

After making a Faith Promise commitment, you still have a part to play. You must be faithful to give as God enables you. That is the real test. Frequently, God supplies what is needed for our Faith Promise, but we conveniently find something else to do with the money. We must be faithful to give what God supplies.

To summarize:
1. Pray for God's direction.
2. Make a realistic assessment of your situation.
3. Obey God's voice in making your commitment.
4. Trust God completely in spite of seeming "impossibilities."
5. Look for God's enablement to meet your Faith Promise.
6. Be faithful to give as God enables you.

Appendix B

Most Asked Questions About Faith Promise

How do you determine what the Faith Promise budget ought to be for your church? What do you do if your church's Faith Promise goal is not reached? How do you receive, administer, and dispense your church's Faith Promise funds?

These, and many other questions, are frequently raised by pastors, missions committee members, and those seriously considering the Faith Promise plan of giving for the first time. This chapter is an attempt to answer the most-asked questions about Faith Promise.

Not everyone who has used the Faith Promise approach will agree totally with the following answers. We tend to frame our answers according to what has worked (or not worked) in our own experience. What a pastor will do in one church, he will alter somewhat when he goes to another church. Each situation calls for different approaches. But there are some general principles that apply in most churches. Let these answers, then, form a general framework from which you can construct a workable Faith Promise plan for yourself or your church.

(The assumption has been made in all these answers that the church has some type of annual missions event. It is in that context that the Faith Promise commitment is most naturally presented and received. Perhaps somewhere there is a church that has a successful Faith Promise emphasis for missions totally apart from any annual missions emphasis. But that would be rare.)

1. I am a pastor. How should I determine the Faith Promise budget for my church?

Do you set the budget before the missions conference? Do you wait until all the Faith Promise cards have been received and totalled, and allow that figure to become the budget?

It is difficult to give a definitive answer because you will find churches that do it both ways with success. It **is** necessary first of all to have a definite budget.

Generally, however, most churches set a budget goal before the commitment cards are received. Some churches make this a prominent part of the missions conference with a big banner announcing the goal; or a thermometer with the goal at the top and a red ribbon to be moved up as the amount comes in. Other churches simply announce an amount that will be needed to cover the budgeted items, and encourage the people to give. The budget goal might also be printed in the bulletin or church newsletter prior to the conference.

The pastor and missions committee meet prior to the missions conference to determine what amount is needed. They review the past year's budget, the missionaries and projects currently supported, and any proposed missionaries and projects they would like to add. A figure is then agreed upon to accomplish this goal.

Other factors should be considered in setting the budget goal.

• Have you had significant numerical growth during the last year in your church? If several new families have joined your church, you would want to increase your budget proportionally. If your church were in a small community that had little or no growth potential, your budget would reflect a smaller increase.

• The economic realities of your people should be considered. A church of 200 people of mostly lower and middle income families will have a smaller budget than a church of 200 people from middle and upper income families. A church of 200 members, many of whom are retired living on social security, will have a much different budget than a church of 200 members of young and middle-aged couples with both partners working.

• To the surprise and delight of many pastors, building programs do not normally adversely affect Faith Promise giving. It is the testimony of countless churches and pastors that their Faith Promise giving did not fall off when a new building program was started. If you are launching a building program, don't cut your Faith Promise budget on the assumption that the money won't come in. One pastor remarked, "After we started using the Faith Promise plan, our people started giving more to the building fund automatically without anything being said." Another pastor commented that their missions giving had increased $50,000 over the previous year, in spite of the big push for building funds to complete a large new sanctuary.

2. What do I do if my church's Faith Promise budget is not reached?

• Go before your people and simply share the facts. Tell them how much came in and how much is lacking to reach the goal.

• Encourage those who did not make a Faith Promise commitment to prayerfully consider making one. (In the average church, about 50% do not make commitments. It seems the larger churches -- with 1,000 members or more -- have a substantial "peripheral fringe" who do not take an active part in the church unless specifically encouraged to do so.)

• Encourage those who did make a Faith Promise to prayerfully consider increasing their commitment. (This does happen from time to time. I talked to a friend who doubled his commitment **twice** during the same missions conference, from $500 to $1,000, and finally $2,000.)

• Ask the people to indicate their response by the following Sunday.

• If, after doing all that, the budget is still not reached, then cutbacks must be made. As a general rule, do not cut missionary support. Cut projects, reserve funds, scholarship funds -- anything but your missionaries' monthly support.

3. How are Faith Promise commitments paid? Weekly? Monthly? Quarterly? Annually?

Usually, churches leave that option up to the individual. It is best, however, if you have these options on the commitment card and encourage the people to indicate, if possible, what they plan to do. This helps the missions treasurer plan for the coming year. Of course, many professionals don't know what their final compensation will be until late in the year. This would apply especially to those in sales with bonus compensation. In that case, a percent of compensation might be indicated.

4. How do you separate and present the different budgets -- local -- missions -- building, etc.?

It is important to keep your missions budget separate from the other budgets. By keeping the missions budget separate, you help people keep proper focus on the importance of missions. A few churches who have especially large missions budgets ($500,000 or more) maintain two separate missions budgets -- a home missions budget and a foreign (overseas) budget. This is almost a necessity when you have a large missions budget.

It is helpful if your budget year for missions is different from your budget year for local operational expenses. The missions budget year is frequently determined by your missions conference date. If you also have a building fund drive, you would not want to schedule the drive too close to your annual missions event.

5. Our church is using the Faith Promise plan for the first time. How do we arrive at a figure for our budget? Are there any general guidelines to follow?

A hint comes from two pastors who have years of experience speaking in missions conferences worldwide. Ken Moon, Pastor of Perry Hall Baptist church, and Bill Boerop, President of World Thrust, both have a rule of thumb which they have arrived at over the years. In general, when a church switches to the Faith Promise plan of giving, the Faith Promise budget the first year is usually double what the regular missions budget was the previous year. Use that as a guide to set your first Faith Promise budget.

6. If the Faith Promise total exceeds our budgeted goal, should we add new missionaries and projects to equal the extra amount that was promised, or wait to see if it really comes in?

A pastor from a strong missions-giving church suggests:

"By all means, add them. I would first check the Reserve Fund in your missions budget. We always had this fund for mission emergencies. Sometimes missionaries have emergency surgery and need extra money. Or they might need some extra funds for special education for their child. Or a missionary needs $1,000 more to cover getting back to the field. So first, I would check to see if this Reserve Fund was strong or if it needed a boost.

"Then we would look at increasing the support of our current missionaries. Maybe we could use the extra money to boost our monthly support for our own mission family.

"Next, we would look at adding new missionaries to our support family. Once a church develops a strong missions program and a large missions budget there are always missionaries contacting the church for support. We keep a file of those and assess them for potential support based on our own goals and mission policy.

"We would also look at our congregation to see if any of our own people were in the process of applying as missionaries soon. We would consider holding some reserve for them to start their support when they were ready.

"We would also look for some projects that needed a boost and give some money to them."

To summarize: Don't sit on the surplus. Use it some way. Get it into circulation.

7. Should we have a cushion built into our missions budget? Suppose our goal is $50,000. Do we set our actual budget for, say, 85% of that amount, just in case it all doesn't come in?

As a general rule, no. Pastors and churches who accept the challenge to support missionaries and projects they feel God wants them to support should commit themselves to that full amount.

8. When do we actually collect the Faith Promise commitment cards?

Before you collect them, it is vitally important several weeks in advance of the conference to begin preparing the people for their Faith Promise commitment. Special announcements can be placed in the bulletin each week. Notice can be made concerning it in the church news sheet, from the pulpit, in each Sunday school class, etc.

Churches use a variety of ways to receive the Faith Promise commitment cards. Some churches wait until the close of the final service of the conference to pass them out, have the people fill them out, and collect them. Other churches place them in the bulletin at the closing service and collect them at the end of the service. Some churches pass out the cards prior to the conference, encouraging the people to pray, fill out their card, and bring it with them to any service during the conference.

Encourage any of your people who will not be present during the conference to mail their card to the missions committee. (You might want to provide a phone number for the convenience of members who travel on business, so they can phone in their Faith Promise commitment.)

The most important thing to remember is to make sure that every single person in your church has a commitment card to fill out. It's also a good idea to have extra cards available at the closing service for any who might have forgotten or misplaced theirs.

9. Should we use a card, an envelope, or something else to indicate the Faith Promise commitment?

Most churches use a single card that has two parts – one to be filled out and turned into the church, the other to be kept as a reminder. Some churches do have a special envelope that has the same information as on the card, but also serves as an envelope for any who might want to make a cash gift at that time. It is entirely possible that you would have visitors in your service who might not feel they wanted to make a Faith Promise commitment but who would like to make a cash gift towards your missions outreach. The envelope provides them that opportunity.

10. Do we announce the total amount of commitments received, and if so, when?

Again, variety is the answer. Some churches collect the commitment cards at the close of the last conference service, quickly add them up, and announce the total before dismissing the service. If you are using a thermometer, the ribbon would be placed at the appropriate number. Other churches collect the cards and announce the total from the pulpit or in the bulletin or weekly church newsletter the following week.

Whatever method is used, it is important to print and announce the total so everyone will know. This knowledge is a good faith builder and encourager.

11. Is there any age limit for making a Faith Promise? Should children be encouraged to make a commitment?

There is no limit. One of the positive benefits about Faith Promise is that anyone of any age and economic standing can make a commitment. Especially do not overlook the children. Even five- and six-year-olds can make a small commitment. Think how that commitment will grow through the years. What better training for faith, trust, commitment, and possible future missionary service than to involve your children early in supporting missions.

12. Should we expect to receive all of the commitment cards by the closing day of the conference?

Usually not. Some people are out of town and will get their cards in later. A few people are still praying about what their commitment should be. Some of those have not yet come to the point of being able to trust God for the amount He is impressing upon them. I talked to a man in Tennessee one Sunday who was having that problem. The missions conference had been three months before but he still had not handed in his commitment card because the Lord was telling him to make a $2,000 commitment, and he was telling the Lord, "That's impossible!"

For at least two Sundays after the conference concludes, encourage the people to fill out their cards and hand them in.

13. Should we have a "cut off" date after which no more cards would be accepted?

Yes. You need some official cut-off time – two to four weeks after the conference. This is necessary so the missions committee can formulate the missions budget for the coming year.

14. Does the missions treasurer keep the Faith Promise commitment cards?

Usually not. Faith Promise is generally presented as being between the individual and God. Therefore, no record is kept of the commitment.

However, some churches do have a line for the person's name as an option if they want to sign it. Some people feel it is not a commitment unless they have signed their name.

A few missions committees do keep the cards. From time to time someone does forget what their commitment was and calls for a reminder.

If the cards are kept, it should be with the understanding that under no circumstances will the missions committee send any type of a "dun" letter asking for the money.

Whichever way you choose to handle this, the commitment cards should definitely have two parts: one to be turned in, and the other to be kept as a reminder.

15. Can a person designate where (s)he wants the Faith Promise used, e.g., for a specific missionary, or missions project?

Usually not. The missions budget would become very unwieldy and difficult to manage if everyone in the church could specify exactly where they wanted their missions money used. The people should be encouraged to give their money to the missions budget of the church, trusting the missions committee and pastoral staff to invest the missions money responsibly, and in line with the church's policies. If members want to designate their giving, then they should be encouraged to send their gifts directly to the missionary's sending organization.

16. What should be included in our church's missions budget? Just support for overseas missionaries, or other things as well?

It is amazing what items show up in a missions budget. One of the important questions to ask is: "How much of our missions budget is being used to reach people cross-culturally in the needy areas of the world?"

Some of the main categories in your missions budget might include:
* Support for missionaries
* Special missions projects.
* A reserve, or emergency fund.
* Missions education in your church.
* A loan fund for schooling for members preparing for full-time mission work.

It is essential to have a missions policy that gives adequate control and priority to these and other matters involving missions money. It is too easy to make money decisions based on emotional appeal -- or because someone is a second cousin of a church member -- or because a missionary "dazzled" the church with snake skins and jungle stories. Policies written down ahead of time give guidance and direction to the missions committee in their stewardship of God's money. ACMC has some excellent material to assist your church in writing its own missions policy.

17. Should our church missions budget be made up entirely of Faith Promise commitments, or should we also have non-Faith Promise money in the missions budget?

Generally, in non-denominational or independent churches, the Faith Promise will comprise the total missions budget for the church. The entire missions budget is the sum of the Faith Promise commitments.

In most denominational churches, the total missions budget usually comes from two sources: the Faith Promise commitments, and the general budget of the church. Frequently, in denominational churches there are two separate missions funds set up. One would be for monies given to the denomination's missions program, and the other strictly for the Faith Promise funds which may be used to support denominational missionaries and projects.

Allow me a personal word of observation. I grew up -- and am still an active member -- in one of the nation's largest denominations. I have been involved in countless missions conferences sponsored by churches of various denominations. Many denominational pastors are particularly hesitant to use the Faith Promise plan of giving for missions because they assume it will automatically reduce the money they take in to meet their own denominational commitments and assessments. Hardly ever is that the case. Almost without exception, the general budget grows, which means churches have adequate funds for their own denominational missions commitments as well.

18. Should I make a Faith Promise if I am heavily in debt?

What should you do if you owe hundreds (or even thousands) of dollars in credit card debt, consolidation loans, or other types of consumer credit? Wouldn't it be more ethical to use as much of your income as possible to pay off your debts, before you start thinking about making a Faith Promise commitment -- or any other giving commitment to missions?

First, it is important to give your tithe to your church even if you are in debt. God expects it, and has promised to honor you as you faithfully return the first portion to Him.

Second, get some Christian counsel regarding how to control your "debt habit," and start **today** putting those principles into practice to reduce and eventually eliminate your debt.

Third, begin with a modest Faith Promise. For someone deeply in debt, a Faith Promise of $50 for the year might seem like an impossible goal. But you will be surprised at how you will be able to meet your commitment -- if you have taken the first two steps. God will honor your faith if you are faithful to tithe and control your spending habits in order to reduce your debt.

* * * * *

And a final question for those who have managed their resources well, have disposable monies in savings and/or investments, and are considering making a Faith Promise commitment:

19. How should I determine the amount of my Faith Promise if I have the ability to write out a substantial check immediately?
A sincere young couple in their late 30s asked me this question. He taught high school math, she took care of the home and three active children. Because they were not enamored with a consumptive lifestyle they lived in a modest home, drove modestly priced cars, and enjoyed a simple standard of living. As a result, even on a teacher's salary, they were able to save money. How, they asked, should they determine their Faith Promise in light of the fact that they could write out a check for several thousand dollars on the spot? And where did "faith" fit into the equation?

Unfortunately, I'm not asked this kind of question often. I suggested to them what I think is a reasonable answer. First, make sure you are tithing at least 10% to your church. Then, prayerfully decide on a percentage of your income (in addition to your tithe) that you would be willing to give towards a Faith Promise, and trust the Lord to enable you to meet that. Have as a second goal increasing that percentage each year. A good place to start would be 2% of your income as your Faith Promise. Then the next year, increase it to 3%. The following year perhaps 5%, and so on. Setting a goal to increase the percentage each year stretches your faith, and encourages meaningful involvement in the Faith Promise over and above your tithe.

Appendix C

How Faith Promise
Worked For One Family

Invariably, when I am a speaker at a missions conference, someone will come up to me and ask, "Where did you serve?" I know they are expecting me to tell them that we were missionaries in Zaire or Tonga or any one of those far-off places that we seem prone to associate with missionary work.

They appear to be a little disappointed when I tell them that I have never served outside the continental U.S., that for thirty-two years I was a pastor in the Western Pennsylvania Conference of the United Methodist Church. I know that, while it is unsaid, what they are thinking is, "Oh, then you weren't a missionary."

Does mileage make a missionary? Is it the distance we have travelled that gives credibility to what we say about missions? Dr. J. T. Seamonds, former missionary to India and long-time Professor of Missions at Asbury Theological Seminary, says, "It is not crossing the sea that makes you a missionary, it is seeing the Cross."

Sometimes I am asked, "Why, if you were not a missionary, are you so interested in missions?" To that I have a stock answer. "I met the Master and read the Book." You can't have met Jesus without wanting to tell the whole world about Him. You can't read the Bible without realizing that missions is something in which every disciple is to be involved. God has different ways for different people to be involved. There are, however, some ways in which all disciples are to be involved. One of those is prayer and another is giving.

Very early in my Christian experience, I realized that God was not going to send me to one of those exotic, mysterious overseas places where missionaries serve. I, like most of you, was destined to spend my life in very ordinary places doing very ordinary things. I also knew that God wanted me to be deeply involved in missions.

One way that He wanted me to be involved was through something called Faith Promise giving. Now, I did not even know that was what it was called when I first started doing it. I only knew that God was asking me to trust Him for $50 to be given to a missions organization. Over the years my wife and I watched that figure grow. First, it was $50, then it was $200, then greater and greater amounts until it became 10% of the Faith Promise budget of the church we were serving. We learned that Faith Promise giving is a growing, learning experience – growing in faith and trust, and learning obedience.

In 1984 we moved from Wilmore, Kentucky to Atlanta, Georgia to join the newly formed Mission Society for United Methodists as its Vice President for Mission Development. For the first time in our lives we were faced with purchasing a home. In the midst of negotiating for the mortgage I felt God saying to me, "Are you willing to commit yourself to giving as much to make Me known to the world as you are prepared to spend to keep a roof over your head?" My first thought was, "Oh, God, You can't be serious. My giving to equal my mortgage payment? Lord, where will I get that kind of money?"

For months I didn't have the courage to broach the subject to my wife. When I finally did, I discovered that she was already farther down the road than I was. I have discovered that when the Lord said, "Two shall become one flesh," He is able to speak to two people, at the same time, about the same subject.

Therefore, at age 65, we started giving as much as we had anticipated our mortgage payment to be, even though our living expenses virtually quadrupled when we moved from Wilmore to Atlanta. God honored that effort.

A little over a year later we went on half salary with the Mission Society. My first thought was, "Lord, are You expecting us to keep on giving at the same level?" His reply was, "Why not keep giving until the money runs out?" My thought was, "That sounds logical." So, we continued our giving at the same level.

Then, 18 months later, we retired from the Mission Society and our income appeared to be further reduced. Again I thought, "Do we continue to give at the same level?" Again, God seemed to be saying, "Has the money run out?"

My wife and I continue to marvel at the way God supplies our needs and enables us to continue giving, even though we have had increased living expenses because of other members of the family sharing our home and because of medical expenses due to health problems. Whatever else we have learned, it certainly includes the truth that God is able and He is faithful. The problem is on our part: hearing Him, trusting Him, obeying Him.

Over the years we have been able to help build schools in Nigeria and hospitals in Zaire, keep planes flying in Papua New Guinea, build shelters for battered women in New Mexico and day care centers for low income families in Pittsburgh, support missionaries and missions projects all around the world in dozens of places. Through prayer and giving we have been able to encircle the globe and enfold the world in our arms and say, "Jesus cares."

We have been able to have an influence for Christ in many lands. Does that not make my wife and me missionaries?[1]

Appendix D

How Faith Promise Worked For One Pastor

Is it really possible to increase your church's missions giving fourfold in just six years, when your church members are convinced they are already stretched to the limit in their giving?

The pastor of a church in the Midwest found out firsthand.

When he came to the church, the attendance was averaging between 200 and 225 each Sunday. At that time the church's missions budget was about $18,000 -- a level it had maintained for several years. The general budget was another $32,000. When the suggestion was made that the church consider having a missions conference and use the Faith Promise plan to help increase missions giving, the response was something short of encouraging. "Pastor, $18,000 is all we can manage" was the general consensus.

Six years later, the missions budget had grown from $18,000 to $76,000 and the general budget from $32,000 to over $120,000. For good measure, the church had paid off all its indebtedness and had a surplus of $40,000 in the general operating budget. (Not bad for a church that by its own admission was "stretched to the limit.")

How did it happen? Allow the pastor to provide the answer in his own words.

"Missions interest and involvement became the life blood of the church. As the people began stretching themselves in faith for missions, spiritual growth and blessing came to individuals; and as that occurred, financial growth came to the church along with deepening spiritual maturity. Our people experienced the truth that 'my God shall supply all your needs.' As we gave out of faith, God blessed us in other areas.

"Before our missions involvement and faith giving for missions, the church struggled just to raise the general budget. There was never enough money. Then, six years later, our missions giving had increased 400%, our general budget had grown 400%, we had paid off the building debts, and had $40,000 surplus in the general fund. There can be no other explanation except God honoring His people when they became serious about missions."

Then the pastor moved to another church. Could the same thing happen again? Let's pick up the story:

"When I went to the new church we were running just a little under 200 in attendance. During my eight years there, the attendance increased to 250, so there was some growth numerically, but not spectacular growth. But what happened to our missions giving **was** spectacular. Before I came, the missions budget was $28,000 and it had been that much for several years. The people didn't think they could give any more, but took pride in the fact of having such a 'large' missions budget. They had not added any new missionaries for support for several years, nor had they increased the support for the few they were supporting. The general budget was about $70,000 at that time.

"The church had been having a missions conference, but they had never set a goal to aim for, nor had they ever used Faith Promise giving. It took us a year or so to make the switch to Faith Promise. The people could not believe the results. In six years the general budget grew from $70,000 to $160,000. And the missions giving grew from $28,000 to $93,000. It just proves that the potential to give much more was there, because our attendance didn't grow all that much. But when the people started stretching themselves in faith, they were able to realize their 'faith potential.' Not only did our general budget more than double, and our missions budget triple, but during that same period we were able to build a new three-story all-purpose building that included a gym, office, and Sunday school rooms.

"I will never forget that first year we took our Faith Promise. I had worked with the missions committee to set a Faith Promise goal. I urged them to set it at $38,000 – about $10,000 more than they had ever given before. With some reluctance they agreed.

"Shortly before the conference began, one of the men talked to me. He had been 'Mr. Missions' in the church for 25 years. He had served as the missions chairman and had been the biggest promoter of missions in the church. He took me aside and said, 'Pastor, I don't want to burst your balloon. I know how eager you are to see this Faith Promise increase our giving to missions. But I know these people! They are conservative and very tight. We will never reach that goal you have set.'

"I don't remember what I said to him. But we had our conference and took up our Faith Promise commitment cards. That same man was in the room with some others as they totalled up the cards that morning. They told me later he had tears streaming down his cheeks as they added the last card, bringing the total to $54,000 – fully $16,000 over the goal. God was faithful to us as our people took their steps of faith."

How do you go about making the change to Faith Promise giving from whatever plan your church is currently using? Here are some of the steps this pastor utilized:

"In each of the churches, we took about two years preparing for the change. In one church we had to change from the unified system, where missions was just one of the items in the general budget, and put the missions money into a separate budget. The people would just designate so much of their tithe to the general budget fund and the rest to the missions budget. We switched both then to the Faith Promise commitment plan.

"During this preparation time we did several things. I gave a lot of time and leadership to it in the first year or so. I talked a lot about it every opportunity I had. But we did other things as well. For example, after the missions committee agreed to move to the Faith Promise plan, I took the entire committee to an all-day missions seminar that had a particular emphasis on Faith Promise. By the end of that seminar, every one of the committee members really 'owned' the Faith Promise concept. They understood it and were committed to it. That was a big help to the whole congregation because the committee could then explain it and answer questions the members might raise. I also got copies of Norm Lewis' book *Triumphal Missionary Ministry in the Local Church* (Back to the Bible Publishers) and gave a copy to everyone on the missions committee, and also to everyone on the deacon board. They read it and we discussed it.

"We also gave everyone in the congregation a tract explaining Faith Promise. And we prepared a sheet of questions and answers about Faith Promise that we mailed to all our members. All this was going on for a year or so leading up to the conference.

"When it came time for the conference, our people had a good understanding of how the Faith Promise worked. Then during the year we kept updating our information. Each week in the bulletin, we printed the average amount that was needed to meet our missions commitment, what the missions giving had been the week before, and how much had been given year-to-date. We also published a monthly church newsletter and we always had updated information about the Faith Promise giving.

"I have seen the results in increased giving for missions using the Faith Promise plan. But, like anything new, it does require a lot of careful planning and preparation if the members are to understand it and participate fully. When the people understand, and make their faith commitment, the results speak for themselves.

"There's nothing like the Faith Promise to generate substantial amounts of money for missions."[1]

Appendix E

Faith Promise Cards

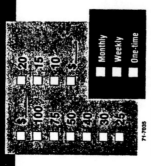

MY MISSIONARY

FAITH PROMISE

As God enables me, I will express my faith and help evangelize the world by giving to the missions program of Church of the Saviour beyond my tithe as I have indicated on this card.

I understand that this faith promise is a covenant between me and God. I will not be asked for payment at any time.

My sincere desire is to commit myself and my financial resources to the cause of world evangelization.

NAME:

$ 20
$ 15
$ 10
$ 5

$ 100
$ 75
$ 50
$ 40
$ 30
$ 25

☐ Monthly
☐ Weekly
☐ One-time

PRAYER
EMPHASIS

Ashland Theological
Seminary
Faith & Charlott Brown
Food for the Hungry
Hollis & Karen Hall
Haven of Rest
Mary Herrin
Randy & Martha Nickel
Tom & Jo Petersburg
Khuna Pakhonrato
Betty Robinson
Stan Scott
Dennis & Ellen Stokes
Shawn & Becky Sullivan
Dave & Martha Vancise
Ron Williams
Harry & Ruth Winslow
Doug & Beth Wright
Jim Young
Emerge Ministry

71-7035

Total Faith Promise $

MY
MISSIONARY
FAITH
PROMISE
REMINDER

I have prom-
ised to give
$ _____
each _____
to Church of
the Saviour's
missions pro-
gram. By mak-
ing this faith
promise I am
expressing my
confidence that
God will sup-
ply the re-
sources to ful-
fill my commit-
ment.

Record
Amount/Date

Eastwood Presbyterian Church

My Faith-Promise for World Evangelization

IN DEPENDENCE UPON GOD I will endeavor to give toward the world-wide Missionary Work of Eastwood Presbyterian Church during the period April 1 of this year through March 31 of next year the amount indicated below.

I understand I WILL NEVER BE ASKED FOR IT. It is a faith agreement between me and God.

My Faith-Promise is_____(annual amount); to be paid as the Lord Provides.

If you like you may make a payment today. If so, please indicate amount enclosed : $_____.

☐ This is a first-time Faith Promise

Name:_____

A Reminder: In dependence upon God, during the coming year. I will trust Him for the amount of $_____.

MY FAITH PROMISE FOR WORLD MISSIONS
First Presbyterian Church
554 McCallie Avenue, Chattanooga, TN 37402

In dependence upon God, I (we) desire to make a faith promise for World Missions to be paid between now and 12/31/89. The total amount of this promise is $_____ to be paid at the rate of $_____ ☐ weekly, ☐ monthly, ☐ annually. Please send me the following number of envelopes to use for payment of my faith promise _____.

Please use my faith promise as follows:
☐ General support of the program . . . . $_____
☐ Specified support of . . . . $_____
☐ Other . . . . $_____

Mr. ☐ Mrs. ☐ Miss ☐_____Date_____
                    (PLEASE PRINT)
Address_____
City_____State_____Zip_____

MY GIFT

Notes

CHAPTER 1: It's All in How You See It
1. *Readers Digest*, February 1988.
2. *Readers Digest*, March 1988.
3. *Consumer Reports*, June 1988.
4. *The Great Omission*, p. 71.

CHAPTER 2: Why Use Faith Promise?
1. *People Magazine*, May 2, 1988.
2. *Evangelical Missions Quarterly*, April 1988.
3. *Faith Promise For World Witness*, Back to the Bible Publishers, 16.
4. *Ibid.*, 26.
5. Paul Smith, *The Sender*, 68.

CHAPTER 3: Miracles Out of the Blue
1. "What's Better Than a Faith Promise Plan," *Eternity*, January 1982, 33.

CHAPTER 4: Lifestyle Giving
1. Ron Blue, *Master Your Money*, 118.
2. *Consumer Reports*, March 1988.

CHAPTER 5: Creative Giving
1. *Atlanta Journal*, March 1, 1989.

CHAPTER 6: History of the Faith Promise
1. A. B. Simpson, *His Life and Work*, 28.
2. *Ibid.*, 98.
3. *Ibid.*, 131.
4. A. W. Tozer, *Wingspread*, 98.
5. A. B. Simpson, *Missionary Messages*, 120.
6. *Ibid.*, 124-125.
7. Paul Smith, *The Senders*, 68.

CHAPTER 8: The "Faith" in Faith Promise
1. Leslie Flynn, *19 Gifts of the Spirit*, 140.
2. Lloyd Ogilvie, *Lord of the Impossible*, 15.
3. Tim Stafford, "Ralph Winter: An Unlikely Revolutionary," *Christianity Today*, September 7, 1984.
4. Chuck Colson, *Loving God*, 37,38.
5. Bob Pierce, Franklin Graham, and Janet Lockerby, *This One Thing I Do*, 52,53.
6. Oswald Chambers, *My Utmost for His Highest,* 304.
7. *Guidepost*, April 1989.

CHAPTER 11: Standard of Living or Standard of Giving?
1. Jack Taylor, *God's Miraculous Plan of Economy*, 30.
2. Ron Blue, *Master Your Money*, 114.
3. Chuck Swindoll, *Strengthening Your Grip*, 76.
4. *U.S. News and World Report*, December 12, 1988, 9.
5. "Plastic Is as Good as Gold," *Readers Digest*, May 1989, 37.
6. "Plastic Power Spells Trouble for Many," *The Birmingham News*, January 22, 1989.
7. Ralph Winter, *Leadership*, Winter 1987, 27.
8. Robertson, McQuilkin, *The Great Omission*, 25.
9. Ron Blue, *Master Your Money*, 120.
10. Chuck Swindoll, *Living Above the Level of Mediocrity*, 43.
11. William Barclay, *The Gospel of Luke*, 223.
12. Chuck Swindoll, *Living Above the Level of Mediocrity*, 116.
13. *Ibid.*, 47.

CHAPTER 12: Misconceptions about Faith Promise
1. Jack Taylor, *God's Miraculous Plan of Economy*, 95.
2. Frank Barker, *Encounters With Jesus*, Victor Books, 103.
3. Ron Blue, *Managing Your Money*, 190.

CHAPTER 13: Beyond the Faith Promise
1. William Barclay, *Letter to Timothy*, 159.
2. Stanley Tam, *God Owns My Business*, Word Publishers, 1969.
3. Leslie B. Flynn, *19 Gifts of the Spirit*, Victor Books, 1974.
4. *Lexington Herald Leader*, December 29, 1988.
5. Sylvia Ronsvalle, *Moody Magazine*, September 1988, 82.
6. Ron Blue, *Master Your Money*, Vol. 1, Number 11, November 1986.
7. *Ibid.*

APPENDIX A: How to Make a Faith Promise

1. Jill Briscoe, Taylor University chapel address, Upland, IN.
2. William Barclay, *The Letters to the Romans*, 69.

APPENDIX C: How Faith Promise Worked for One Family
1. Testimony by V. E. Maybray, "We Serve in Many Lands!" Appeared in abbreviated form in *Mission Advocate*, April 1989, published by the Mission Society for United Methodist, P.O. Box 11103, Decatur, Georgia 30031, edited by Julia Williams.

APPENDIX D: How Faith Promise Worked for One Pastor
1. Personal interview with Rev. Al Tedder, pastor of the Faith Church, St. Petersburg, Florida.

APPENDIX E: Samples of Faith Promise Commitment Cards